A Time
FOR EVERY PURPOSE

by Barbara Taylor Woodall

Copyright © 2015 by Barbara Taylor Woodall
All Rights Reserved. No part of this book may be reproduced or transmitted in any form or by any means, electronic or mechanical, including photocopying, recording or by any information storage or retrieval system, without permission in writing from the author or publisher.

First Edition 2015

Books By Barbara Taylor Woodall
"It's Not My Mountain Anymore," 2011

Layout: Amy Ammons Garza
Photography: Barbara Taylor Woodall

Publisher:
Catch the Spirit of Appalachia, Inc.
Imprint of: Ammons Communications
SAN NO. 8 5 1 – 0 8 8 1
29 Regal Avenue • Sylva, North Carolina 28779 •
Phone/fax: (828) 631-4587

Library of Congress Control Number: 2015942189

ISBN No. 978-0-9908766-8-7

PRINTED IN THE UNITED STATES OF AMERICA

Dedication

I dedicate this book to all those who encouraged my feeble efforts to tackle a second book. Many of you I have not met yet. Please know how much I value your support.

Acknowledgements

I gratefully acknowledge the hands-on assistance and contributions of Pat Rogers, Laurie Brunson Altieri, Ann Henslee Moore, Margie Bennett, Bob Justus, Cherie Faircloth, Melissa Woodall, Jean Nelson, and Susie Tanner Swanson. You all dedicated your time and energy to make this book a reality.

I am especially grateful to Eliot Wigginton without whom I and others might not have amounted to a hill of beans. He often said, "Life isn't worth living until you bet everything you have on something you believe in and go for broke."

To my brothers Edward and Ellis Taylor I give heartfelt thanks for helping me remember seasons of the past.

I thank Amy Ammons Garza for her contributions and Doreyl Ammons Cain for creating the beautiful cover of *A Time For Every Purpose*. I will be forever grateful to these precious sisters for founding Catch the Spirit of Appalachia and providing me the opportunity to publish my bestselling first book *It's Not My Mountain Anymore* as well as this book.

Special thanks to the good Lord who gave us the greatest Book and common sense to understand it. As we each pass through the seasons of life, I'm grateful we can share the constant surprises.

Contents

Introduction..07

CHAPTER

1   A Time To Be Born, And A Time To Die..........11
2   A Time To plant, And A Time To
       Pluck Up That Which Was Planted................27
3   A Time To Kill, And A Time To Heal...............36
4   A Time to Break Down, And A Time
       To Build Up..45
5   A Time To Weep, And A Time To Laugh..........58
6   A Time To Mourn, And A Time To Dance........65
7   A Time To Cast Away Stones, And A Time
       To Gather Stones Together............................72
8   A Time To Embrace, And A Time
       To Refrain From Embracing........................ 86
9   A Time To Get, And A Time To Lose...............91
10   A Time To Keep, And A Time
       To Cast Away...98
11   A Time To Rend, And A Time To Sew............106
12   A Time To Keep Silent,
       And A Time To Speak.................................114
13   A Time To Love, And A Time To Hate............121
14   A Time Of War, And a Time Of Peace............128

Conclusion...136
About the Author...139

Introduction

"To everything there is a season, and a time to every purpose under the heaven: A time to be born, and a time to die; a time to plant, and a time to pluck up that which is planted; A time to kill, and a time to heal; a time to break down, and a time to build up; A time to weep, and a time to laugh; A time to mourn, and a time to dance; A time to cast away stones, and a time to gather stones together; A time to embrace and a time to refrain from embracing. A time to get, and a time to lose; a time to keep and a time to cast away; A time to rend, and a time to sew; a time to keep silence, and a time to speak; A time to love and a time to hate; A time of war, and a time of peace."
—Ecclesiastes 3:1-8 (KJV)

Those who live long enough on life's timed journey will experience all of the twenty-eight seasons described by Solomon in the book of Ecclesiastes. Time is duration set forth by measures, seasons created by God that allow us to experience His perfect plan and fulfill our role in its development. Time is the circle from which God is bringing all things unto Himself.

According to Ed Vallowe, author of *Biblical Mathematics Keys to Scripture Numerics*, the number twenty-eight depicts eternity. Eternity is different from time. It is a state of absolute timelessness and is part of the nature of God.

I treasure time spent in the Georgia mountains amidst fenceless trails and ever-changing scenes.

When I feel the need to abate all tomorrows and loose the chains that often bind my mind, I escape to nature where I am compelled to be still and know that He is God.

Moss-covered logs are nature's rest areas amidst dew-kissed surroundings. Dew never falls on restless forests or on reeling souls. In the midst of the fair calmness of nature, the soul can absorb priceless, tender moments in a state where death and decay are unnoticed. The only sound I hear is flowing creek waters sending sweet freedom notes through the trees like music that penetrates one's very being.

Nature decorates our area with four distinct seasons. Autumn is my favorite, and the crowning glory of the four because it teaches the end is more beautiful than the beginning. Forest paths of my ancestors become streets of gold covered by fallen leaves that crunch underfoot, and they remind me how fragile heritage is. All four seasons embrace creation and cloak us in gowns of learning as nature teaches mighty lessons along life's pathways.

The timepiece on my arm is a reminder of precious time. A setting sun announces the end of each day. A beating pulse echoes time's value. The perfect flowers bow their heads and wither away.

Moments spent with others include appointed times listed in Ecclesiastes. Time is a most precious gift that I can give to others. It never stands still. Neither does our young grandson, Christopher.

No matter what time of day it is, the sound of my approaching golf cart disrupts all Christopher's previous activities. He rears his carrot-top head to look

A Time for Every Purpose

from his porch with great expectation. Suddenly his small face lights up like a thousand candles. He begins to jump up and down in total exuberance, running the length of the porch peeking between the railings. Tiny hands reach through the pickets making rapid "come get me" motions. My nearing causes our hearts to flutter like the wings of a baby bird. His eyes reflect the purest love on earth. Father allows the two of us to experience a season of unconditional love. The Oak Ridge Boys sum up a child's value in their song, "Thank God for kids, there's magic for a while. A special kind of sunshine in a smile. Do you ever stop to think or wonder why the nearest thing to heaven is a child?"

Christopher and I enjoy "a time to laugh, a time to dance, a time to gather stones together, a time to embrace, a time to get, a time to keep and a time to love."

I am grateful the twenty-eight appointed seasons listed above are in Divine hands. Appointed times cannot be hastened, delayed or changed. Time teaches me patience, and endurance. Each season is the beginning of new experiences.

Chapter 1

A Time to be Born, and a Time to Die

Life is by divine appointment. Each creature is wonderfully made according to God's purpose and for His pleasure. We are planted on earth to fulfill His destiny for us. Seven generations of my family were planted in these ancient mountains to live amidst the glorious beauty. We didn't need a calendar in the north Georgia mountains where I was born, to tell us appointed seasons had arrived. The seasons of life are keenly experienced in my Georgia mountain homeland. Each appointed time brings change and marks God's perfect timing for all creation.

Spring signals the birth and youth of life. Summer brings the mid-season, the halfway mark of a year in life's circle. The long days summer leaves behind turn into crisp autumns. Autumn turns into winter, a sign the end of another passing year has arrived.

The harsh breath of winter's north wind sweeps across fields and pastures leaving a feathery glaze of white frost on every twig and blade. Soft mountain soil turns hard as rock, and Kelly's Creek becomes framed with snow and icicles hanging like big clothespins holding mountain laurel leaves in place. The coldness goes plumb to the bone like a witch's bosom in a brass brassiere.

Kelly's Creek

Sounds of Mama loading the firebox in the end of her wood cook stove signaled the birth of a new day. From my tiny bedroom, I could hear her breaking ice in the water buckets with a rolling pin on the back porch. A squeaking door hinge told she was bringing the water bucket inside to heat it on the stove. After she washed her hands in the warmed water, she sifted about two pounds of White Lily flour into a tan wooden bowl. Unclothing the top of a five-gallon churn sitting in the corner, her fingers scooped lard she had rendered in November and now added to the flour. Next, she poured risen whey from a gallon jar of fresh buttermilk, then poured the thicker milk into the flour and lard mixture to work the dough for biscuits. Once she finished kneading the soft dough, she pinched off portions the size of a cat's head to shape into "cathead biscuits." A piping hot pan of morning delights soon emerged from the oven. Added to the morning feast were fried sausage, cream gravy, and hot buttered applesauce.

Outside, wood smoke moved slowly upward until it dropped and settled close to the ground, mingling with falling snow.

A bone chilling wind blew thin dustings of white powder underneath our weather-cracked front door. Sometimes it whistled down the rock chimney sending gray smoke through the house.

A Time for Every Purpose

Mama said, "Darn th' luck t' hell, I get one gaum (mess) cleaned up and here comes another 'en! Th' house is full of smoke and you can't catch one spoonful!" She grabbed two empty dishpans to fan it back outside. It looked like we were going off on a train.

We waited long winter days near the warmth of the mud-daubed fireplace. At night, flickers from the fire created color wheels of amber and glowed against a plank ceiling as I imagined watching an artist paint pictures on a color television screen, while waiting on the spring thaw.

Since the beginning of time, spring has been a picture of renewed hope in new life. Gently the earth is touched by warm sunbeams to awaken the forests. I imagine it yawning and stretching like Homer the cat coming out of his warm bed near the stove. Millions of tender green shoots wiggle and push through rich soil breaking winter's iron grip. Hints of tiny leaves peek through weathered tree limbs and around old locust fence posts covered with layers of aging moss. New grass appears among tiny blue flowers near the springhouse and in the pasture. All nature opens her bright eyes and every creature seems to rejoice and reach for the sky.

Ol' Heif, the family cow, began to shed her thick winter coat. She no longer needed to be jacked up above the snow at milking time.

She had been dry for about six weeks, and all swelled up. At the appointed time, Ol' Heif slipped off, and the constant ringing of her rusty bell ceased. Soon she reappeared from the thickets, nudging and licking a red and white wobbling calf. Her bawl gained our attention as they moved toward the barn.

Granny Lou proudly said, "Look yonder! Ol' Heif has freshened. She scratched out a calf from under a rock! Now, don't you young'uns be foolin' with that calf. Ol' Heif will be on th' fight; stay away from the barn. That cow will lunge at you; she means business."

Dad let the calf run with Ol' Heif for three days before he separated them. The calf was housed in a separate barn stall because it would take all the milk. A mournful, lonesome bawl echoed all day and through the night as Ol' Heif paced the field searching for her beloved. Her grieving heart deeply saddened me.

Twice a day, Dad turned the calf into the milking stable for feedings. White foam leaked from its mouth as it sucked two teats on the left side, while Dad milked the two on the right side. Often he squirted warm milk into lurking cat mouths, and then watched as they cleaned their faces.

Adding to spring scenes, two robins sat on the locust fence rails, observing in all directions. They were considering the best nesting place. Each bird busied itself with song, as the pair worked together weaving a home for their young under the shelter of sturdy but weathered barn eaves. I watched as they lifted straws, twigs and fallen hairs from the horse's tail without harming a speck of landscape. It seemed they made a million trips back and forth carefully weaving each piece in perfect order, preparing for their

A Time for Every Purpose

appointed times. Lined with love and commitment, their nest held more than tiny eggs.

Sassy hens clucked and paced the barnyard ignoring the cocky rooster's need for attention. They searched for a place of solace to steal away and build nests to hold their brood. A common riddle about eggs was repeated each spring: "It has no windows, it has no doors. When inside comes out, it returns no more."

Even before the diddlers hatched, mama hens wrote their laws with various cluck commands within each one. After 21 days of almost motionless, constant attention yellow chicks began to peck their way out of eggshells into a new world of light, tasty worms and adventure. Under watchful eyes and soft-feathered breasts, the protected chicks felt mama's every heartbeat and the warmth of spring love.

The hens proudly reappeared in the barnyard with fluffy broods, their pride and joy. They constantly clucked and scratched the dirt looking for food. A hen is a good example of providing for the needs of a family.

Spring fever affected all creation with sweet smells and new births. Granny Lou, guided by her nose, headed up the hill looking for sassafras trees. They were easy to spot by their bright yellow buds shining like gold on the hillsides. The leaves are shaped like mittens. It was fun to "try on" a pair. Tender sweet birch twigs made dandy chewing gum and added to the season. The trees could also be tapped for birch beer.

After a hard winter, Granny Lou believed our blood needed renewing and thought if we drank sassafras tea in March, we would be healthy all year. We didn't know it back then, but sassafras is a natural blood thinner.

Her apron pockets would budge with twigs, bark, and roots she had cut small enough to fit into a boiling pot. Aromas from the kitchen smelled like root beer as the tea simmered to shades of brown. Finally, Granny Lou reached for the sugar sack to sweeten the brew, signaling our annual dose of spring tonic was on its way.

Her knowledge was priceless, and matched the abundance of leaves, roots, and herbs that filled spring woodlands.

We got our vitamins from all sorts of spring greens growing in lush fields. One was pokeweed. When it reached about six inches high, a community call went forth. "Put up your dogs, we don't want any yellow leaves!"

After Granny Lou gathered a mess of poke sallet, she washed it several times, and then parboiled the leaves twice. Finally, she fried it in an iron skillet with hog grease. Poke sallet was topped with hard-boiled eggs for a tasty and colorful combination.

Like springtime, our lives have seasons of renewal and rebirth. We grow and change together on life's journey.

Our summer and fall of youth was spent in bright sunshine spilling through mountain trees that filled us with the deep greenness of life. Winter was sure to follow, shaking members of creation with icy storms. Weak twigs and branches are broken by strong winds and return to the earth. Just as sure as we are born, there is an appointed time to drop our frail flesh bodies.

~ ~ ~

Life is measured even before we were born. Each of our footsteps are counted by the Lord and directed from before the womb to beyond the grave. Like the winding creeks that flow through the coves and the woodland of these mountains, life winds its way through the paths of seasons. His timing for our coming and going is perfectly planned.

The first sound I hear each morning filtering through the still mountain air is the mystery of flowing creek waters. Their motions remind me of life's ever-winding journey. Kelly's Creek, where we live, has its origin high on the mountain. Finger-size trickles ooze from underneath a huge ancient rock making their way downward through bracken ferns, rocks, and fallen trees. The trickles become streams that mingle and flow freely down rough mountain terrain. They gain strength by volume and speed, as clear cascades tumble downward crashing against boundaries and obstacles along its path. Nothing can stop water's pre-determined path.

Seasons change the character and form of the creek. In the spring, banks are lined with fresh green mints, healing herbs, and groves of colorful wildflowers that add to the great calmness fed by the nourishing waters. In the heat of summer, mist from the creek waters clings to overhanging limbs and leaves helping to keep the environment cool. In the winter, that same mist changes to ice and holds nature in a frozen claw until warming rays of sunshine slowly change the scene into vapor that is gathered into clouds high above the mountain ranges.

I believe when our earthly journey is over, like waters, we merely change our form. At the appointed time, we simply drop painful flesh bodies and the spiritual body that already resides inside us comes forth. People generally associate death with the end, but I believe it is a new beginning in a higher realm just like the end of a stream's path that spills into a much deeper source.

Often at funerals, we hear the Bible text, "It is appointed unto man once to die." Most people equate this to the grave. I ain't no preacher, but I believe Christ defeated death. His words, "Ye shall never die" are a wonderful reality. Fear has torment. People fear things they do not understand. Learning promotes understanding that dispels fear.

My brother Ernest lived with his wife in a modest

house just across the road on a part of Dad's property very near to a peaceful waterfall. Illiteracy caused by a learning disability held him in great bondage, forcing him to rely on the words of others. He had an amazing memory that helped him keep full time jobs to support his family. After Ernest retired from driving trucks, I grew accustomed to his regular morning visits. Generally, he filled his vacant time helping me piddle with outside chores. We mended fence lines, picked blackberries, gardened, cut grass, or stacked firewood, depending on the season. He was good company.

In April of 2012, I noticed his steps became slower on the short journey to his mailbox. Often he steadied himself alongside my house, making his way onto the porch with a handful of mail. One day we were patching holes in our shared driveway when he staggered a bit while mixing cement in Dad's old wheelbarrow. I assumed his blood sugar level had dropped and quickly tanked him up on sweet iced tea, to no avail.

Soon afterwards, medical testing revealed a tumor in his brain. The doctor was brutally honest: "Cancer is spreading like letting a horse out of a barn." It is hard to be brave when cancer shatters families and hearts. For a moment, our world stopped turning. The waterfall near his home seemed to freeze in motion in a land of grief. Rumbles like earthquakes from deep within rattled and cracked our souls. I thought about the earth opening her mouth to swallow up my brother like the dust from which we were created. I offered encouragement. . . that "a horse can be roped and bound," assuring Ernest, he was not alone.

The life-rich foliage of our youth was suddenly stripped bare like naked trees shaken by howling winter winds on the mountainside.

Sometimes, gray clouds overcome bright blue skies. Cold seasons teach lessons in life. In the winter, tree branches have no shade to shadow the earth. Each tree must endure the cold. Yet, there is unseen life and unseen strength in the steel gray mountains.

A Time for Every Purpose

Rich tree sap flows downward to settle in strong roots holding mountains together. Cold seasons are times of rest and preparation. These are the times when testing, trials and tribulations pelt us like silver sleet and beat upon our gray barrenness that we might bloom, blossom, and bring forth in due season.

My words of encouragement to Ernest seemed to fall on deaf ears. He became totally consumed with worry. Mama always said, "I'd rather be sick than worried." There is a lot of truth in her words. His endless agony seemed worse than the cancers. It appeared to me that my brother stopped living the day of the diagnosis.

His wife Bessie Ann, a born caregiver, has a heart as soft as feathers. In the late afternoons, she played the piano. The sounds of easy and gentle hymns flowed from their open window, softening the air of grief. She played the old tunes, the ones you never tire of hearing, like "Amazing Grace" and "Blessed Assurance." Music soothes the soul, cheers heavy hearts, and sweetens a grim atmosphere. I made it a point to spend time with Ernest and Bessie Ann. The three of us sat on their porch talking and laughing in the evenings. Laughter is good medicine, so I always looked for humorous topics to share.

In time, our conversations turned towards the Bible. We rarely discussed beliefs until this appointed time. As we sat on the porch, Ernest began to ask questions. I deeply valued his trust. Many times when he came to visit, he found me surrounded with Bible study aids. He took note of the duct tape holding my personal Bible together and the many scribbles and highlights on each page. Once he asked, "How do you tell your words from God's words?"

We recalled as young'uns, the radio was tuned to religious broadcasts each Sunday. Hell fire, and damnation voices filled our home with fear. Thundering voices of preachers splattered on the walls and stuck on the pine splintered planks. Their words painted horror images in our young minds of God burning people like bacon on a stick. As Ernest now listened intensely, I asked, "Do you think a spirit or a soul could feel physical pain or be destroyed?"

He said, "No, they cannot be harmed in the hottest stove in hell."

I shared my belief that the concept of hell, fire and brimstone, did not come from a loving God. Then, I read and explained several scriptures from the book of Jeremiah that state it never entered God's mind to burn His children. Eternal torture is based on misunderstanding and man-made doctrines. The fire of God melts away our imperfections with Divine love. Ernest liked that idea.

Spiritual food is like food at the supper table. Everyone has an individual appetite. As often as Ernest asked, I answered the best I could.

I shared with him my belief that heaven was not a golden box located somewhere in outer space, filled with winged beings walking on streets of gold, or peering through pearly gates. I believe to walk on streets of gold means to walk with God, and it is not reserved for someday when we all get to heaven. The pearly gates represent each of His children, who are pearls of great price.

A Time for Every Purpose

Ernest and I agreed, if heaven does not favor the Appalachian Mountains, somebody will have to chain us up; else we will climb over a cloud and come home! Religion had heaped loads of guilt on his weary heart, truth set him free. A veil of cloudy bondage slowly lifted like fog from his eyes.

I shared an example in nature with Ernest that gave him extra comfort. Mountain trees become decorated with strange, white ornaments as hungry caterpillars lose their appetite for earthly goods and begin to spin tight, silky tents underneath fading green leaves. They appear to be hopelessly burying themselves in a dark cocoon, but deep within each caterpillar's being is an undeniable predestination to fly. The entire appointed process cannot be hastened. Pressure builds inside the ugly cocoon's prison like our trials and tribulations, sickness and pain, as the

caterpillar begins to change form. A beautiful butterfly finally breaks forth to untold freedom. Ernest gained courage and peace from truths of nature.

My brother's appointed time to drop his flesh body was drawing near. A few days before his transition, Ernest said when he closed his eyes he saw a bright light, and so radiant it could only be seen with his eyes closed. The Bible describes God as Light. On his appointed day, and only moments away from his transition, Ernest told his family he loved them, winked at our sister, Betty, and reached forth his hand in a farewell gesture. Then, in the twinkling of an eye, he reached up as if to grasp an unseen hand. His spirit took flight like a butterfly escaping from a cocoon.

Lightness filled the room as the sound of the

creek waters seemed to magnify in my ears. Ernest's process of toil on earth ceased, and his transition was complete, November 26, 2012-- the day after Thanksgiving.

Like the flowing waters of Kelly's Creek, he now rests in an ocean filled with Divine love. Seven months of suffering ended. Seven in Bible numbers means spiritual perfection. Ernest moved from being planted by the waters of Kelly's Creek to being planted in the waters of everlasting life.

Chapter 2

A Time to Plant, and A Time to Pluck up That Which is Planted

In God's seasons, timing is everything. Planting and harvesting our crops depended on His wisdom and determined our bounty for the coming year. The same holds true for the bounty in our everyday lives.

In these hills are grateful hearts of those born here and those who got here as fast as they could seeking the beauty and solace of mountain pastures. Both have buried seeds of belonging, to nurture through seasons. There is wisdom in the words, "Ye reap what ye sow." A time to pluck up that which is planted is God's perfect plan to reap what we sow in the fields of life. There can be no harvest unless seeds are planted in His good earth. Likewise, encouraging words and acts of kindness bring forth good fruits from our labor when planted in fertile hearts.

Barren fields in the Georgia mountains lay silent through the dead of winter as the land rests. Old stalks and weeds stand in the frozen rows like naked soldiers. Seeds sleeping in withered brown pods are shaken and scattered by the wind into every crack and

A Time for Every Purpose

crevice in the cold earth. Until the magic of warm yellow sunbeams touch the new season and nourishing spring rains fall from the heavens to prepare the ground, no seed will germinate.

Dad spent the early days of spring at the barn preparing for a time to plant. He re-conditioned the hoes, shovels, pitchforks, axes and rakes. Old handles were replaced with hewn white hickory he soaked in the creek to swell the wood for a tight fit. An old sharpening wheel kept tools in mint condition. It was mounted on a wooden box that held water. My brothers toted buckets of water from the creek to fill the box. A turning handle was mounted in the center of the stone. Slowly, I turned the handle as Dad held tools against the smooth white stone. Colorful sparks lit up the area like a 4th of July celebration as metal flakes fell into the water box. The stone put a nice edge on the farm tools.

Cobwebs and barn dust were swept from resting plows, and the mule harness was checked for cracks and breaks. Dad did his homework in The Farmer's Almanac to determine dates to plow and plant. My ancestors believed strongly that the heavens direct our path and the stars speak without words through signs and seasons.

According to the Bible, their teachings are "*More to be desired than gold, yea, than much fine gold: sweeter also than*

honey and the honeycomb. Moreover by them is thy servant warned: and in keeping of them there is great reward." —Psalms 19:10-11(KJV)

When the Zodiac signs were in the head, or Aries, Dad began cultivating the soil. This sign was pictured on the planting calendar as a ram. He waited until the signs changed to Taurus the bull, with the signs in the neck, to plant root crops like potatoes. Never did he plant potatoes when the signs were in Pisces, or the feet, saying "All ye git is a'crop of marbles about the size of toes. It's all vines and no 'taters." The best potato crops were planted on the dark nights of the moon, which is the first new moon in March or April.

He selected seed corn ears from last year's crop stored in the small crib attached to the end of the barn. It was shelled by hand because the corn sheller crushed the heart in the seeds. After much preparation, the womb of the earth was now ready to receive seed.

At the appointed time, hard-shelled casings start to crack open, and the heart of the seed begins to sprout new life.

A time to plant also included planting seeds of wisdom in the minds of younger generations. I have often heard, "Never plant corn when th' signs are in th' heart. Black specks will take over and ruin your crop. Plant beans when th' signs are in th' arms if you want full hulls. Th' best time t' cut brush is in August before the sap falls. There won't be enough sap returned to th' stump to sprout new limbs."

My folks were never short on humor or tall tales. I grew up hearing, "Plant peppers when you're good and mad if you want 'em t' be hot.

"Never plant onions above your 'tater patch. They will get in the eyes of the 'tater and wash your crop away!

"It's dangerous t' plant watermelons. If the cow breaks one, she will surely drown. You can make a fishpond from half a rind.

"Turnips grow so big; they crack the ground like an earthquake. Locust fences fall down and ye have t' use a cross-cut saw t' slice 'em for cooking."

Jokes were played on children, too, like, "Plant ye a row of cucklebur seeds t' grow some porcupines or a row of jelly beans for a sweet harvest."

Dad kept a constant check on the crops. Pests were discouraged by sprinkling dew-kissed plants with wood ashes that were saved in a pile from the fireplace.

By late August, green treetops framed a deep blue sky. Hints of kaleidoscope colors began to appear in a few turning leaves, signaling the appointed time to pluck up the harvest.

Full crops waved in ripening fields moved by dry breezes. Large yellow squash blooms fed the bees and butterflies that flew overhead. Rows of okra, beans, beets, peas, potatoes, onions, sweet potatoes, cucumbers, and peppers were nearing harvest time.

Baskets of red ripe tomatoes rested on the end of the porch until Mama began processing them into juice and soup. Four or five bushels of white half-runner beans took much time and attention. If we picked peas prior to helping with the beans, Mama would jest, "Don't you dabble in these beans with 'pee' on your hands." Some beans were strung together with a large threaded darning needle, and then hung over the rafters to dry. We called these shuck beans or leather britches. In the winter, Mama pulled two or three strands from the rafter. First, she washed them several times then put them in a boiling pot of water. She poured off the first boil to insure extra cleanliness. During the second boil, she threw in a chunk of meat and onions that simmered all day. Leather britches sure beat snowballs on the supper table.

Beans Used with permission
Sautee Nacoochee Center

Sometimes the crops came in so fast the family was rushed for time and often worked late into the night. Long evenings of picking, stringing, breaking, washing, rinsing, packing, salting and canning was hard work, but well worth the reward. Filled Mason jars swayed gray, splintered shelves in the can house like a general store.

Orchard branches bent low to the earth loaded with shiny fruits waiting to become golden applesauce or canned peach slices. Dad never picked fruit on the new moon, saying it would rot. Apples were sliced and air-dried before storing them for the winter in a poke. The goodness of harvest was seen, tasted, touched, and felt throughout the farm.

Occasionally Aunt Blanche Harkins came to the house to make a deal with my brothers. She owned an old reel type lawn mower with one wooden handle she could not push through her tall grass. She prepared half-moon apple pie treats in exchange for labor. The boys went to her house to cut grass and she went to Mama's kitchen.

First, she emptied and washed about a quart of dried apples in a pan. Next, she cooked them with a little water until tender enough to mash with a fork. Then, about a cup of sugar and spice to taste was added to the mixture. Aunt Blanche spooned the mixture into prepared crusts about the size of a hand; next, she flipped and sealed the dough with the end of a fork. Heavenly scents ascended from an iron skillet with great temptation to eat all my brothers' reward. They were good enough to make you run out on the porch and holler.

Cabbage was one of the last vegetables added to our food winter food supply. Firm white heads waited for the new moon to rise over mellow fields decorated with thousands of colorful morning glory flowers.

As Mama chopped the cabbage to fit into pickling churns, she often sang an old Irish folk song about a drunkard who came home questioning evidence of his wife's lover.

> *"Well, I came home the other night*
> *Just drunk as I could be*
> *Found a head on my pillow*
> *Where my head ought to be*
> *Now, come my little wifey*
> *Explain yourself to me*
> *How come that head on my pillow*
> *Where my head ought to be?*
> *Well, you blind old fool, you drunken old fool*
> *Can't you never see?*
> *That's just a cabbage head*
> *my granny gave to me*
> *Well, I've traveled this world over*
> *A hundred miles or more*
> *but whiskers on a cabbage head*
> *I never did see before"*

  Mama placed layers of chopped, salted cabbage in a clay five-gallon churn. A clean round rock taken from the creek bed was placed on top of the mixture to hold it under the brine. She tied a white cloth around the top, and then capped it with a plate. My brother toted the heavy churn to the can house. After ten days of fermentation, she canned the kraut to keep it brittle.

  Chimney smoke from the season's first fires scented mountain air and settled over drying fields as the last wagon loaded with corn creaked and squeaked towards the old barn.

  Later, fodder (dried corn blades) was pulled and

tied to cornstalks to feed the cattle during the winter. Corn shocks dotted fields like warm wigwams. They made dandy playgrounds for young'uns.

Leaning on his crutches, Grandpa said, "Leave

one or two shocks in th' field for wild critters t' eat this winter."

A time to pluck up was a time of thanksgiving and a joyous period to celebrate hard work and the promise of a full winter's table that included free-range chickens, wild game and pork.

Chapter 3

A Time To Kill, and A Time to Heal

A time to kill has nothing to do with murder. The Bible forbids criminal homicide. A slayer not only takes a life, but the potential for future generations is wiped out.

There is an appointed time to put meat on the table. Sometime in late May, when the plantain weeds were tall enough to pull for pig feed, Dad handed my brothers $5.00 and a couple of tow sacks, then sent them to the Mud Creek community in search of Hampshire pigs. Mama called them "sweater pigs" because they had a white stripe over each shoulder and down their front legs.

The hog farmer was a humorous mountain man with a gentle spirit and twinkling blue eyes that welcomed my brothers into his presence. His garden was surrounded with a shaky paling fence that offered some protection from his free-ranged hogs.

He was dressed in oversized brown Duck Head coveralls held in place by a tightly buckled leather belt. His worn, weather-cracked boots were soaked with water, but that did not dampen the broad grin

across his slim face. The farmer remembered that Dad didn't want a pig whose tail curled to the left, because he believed it would not fatten well. The farmer shelled an ear of corn, enticing the piglets near. He grabbed two pigs by their trotters and stuck them in the sacks; then my brothers toted them home. They turned them loose in a crude hog pen made from sawmill slabs, far away from Mama's clothesline. Within a few months, the piglets turned into fat hogs as a time to kill approached.

Clyde Oliver lived with his aging brother about a mile from our house in a run-down shack. His skinny-as-a-rail-body bore marks of neglect from years of abuse wrought by his constant companion, a pint of white lightning. Salt and pepper hair covered dirty ears that held in place an old battered railroad cap. Mama said, "He boogers at soap an' water. Somebody he know'd musta got killed with it."

He lived half-lit and sometimes pitched sop drunks. It was common to find his small frame curled up like a cat, passed out in the barn, under a tree or in the woodshed. One day he wandered into the hog lot and lay down with the sows. After sobering up he said, "I was rubbin' that ole sow's belly and wondering why Maude had so many buttons on her gown!"

In November, when the mountain air become chilled and heavy frost covered our isolated world like sparkling diamonds in morning sunlight, my folks began sharpening butcher knives on a whetting stone. They never sharpened objects on Sunday, believing someone would get cut before the week was out. Dad tested the knives for razor sharpness by shaving the hair off of small sections of his arm.

Outside, he prepared two fifty-five gallon scalding barrels that were filled with creek water and set in place on a shaky, rock furnace.

Inside, Mama washed and dried big processing pots and pans. Crates of canning jars rattled together as we toted them from the can house for washing and sanitizing. That night, Dad sat in a wooden chair cocked up against a splintered pine wall near the firelight pondering the next day's work. He talked about phases of the moon and turned worn pages in the Farmer's Almanac, double-checking the signs.

Early the next morning, Dad picked up the slop bucket on the back porch filled with table scraps for the fattened hog's final meal. When he returned from the hog pen, he reached for the rifle above the fireplace. That's when I became scarce, because "gory land" was upon us.

The sound of the rifle at the hog pen followed by bloody trails to the scalding barrels sickened me. The smell of steaming hot water poured on the carcasses tainted the air. I could hear Dad swinging the double-bitted ax, chopping up sections of meat and dreaded bloody portions brought into the kitchen for processing. Four big hams, shoulders and middlin' meats were laid on crude smokehouse shelves and salted down for curing.

Mama washed and carefully inspected each piece of meat that passed through the kitchen. Portions were cut for processing. The sausage was ground and seasoned with dried sage and pepper. Slowly, jars were filled with meat and grease to the brim. Chunks of fat were rendered into snow-white lard and stored in a churn. Cracklings are the by-products from rendered lard. All true Appalachians know the luxury of crackling cornbread. Mama never measured ingredients, but she took about two cups of sifted, old-timey cornmeal and added one-quarter cup of lard or bacon grease and one-teaspoon salt. Next, she put in a pinch of baking soda and poured about two cups of buttermilk into the mixture. Lastly, she added a cup of fresh cracklings.

The batter was poured into a greased iron skillet and baked at 450 degrees for about 30 minutes. When she turned the fresh dodger of bread onto a cooling board, the delicious aroma filled the whole house. I forgot about "gory days" for a while. We made many of a meal off that, an onion and a glass of sweet milk.

A Time for Every Purpose

Sometimes, I gander (look) down the road at the old, weathered smokehouse and recall a time to kill. Frozen memories begin to thaw like ice near a fire, of Dad entering to turn the meat or to make cuts for supper. His faded bib overalls swallowed his thin, lanky frame. The hind pockets hung closely together and looked like they were shaking hands.

Mountain families also depended on wild game as a source of food well into the 20th century. Many young'uns grew up learning to hunt. In fact, school was often skipped during deer season. Hunting was not vital to my family, but one of my brothers liked the sport, and it kept him busy training hunting dogs.

Mama said, "There ain't no sport to it until the

varmints get a gun."

Slaying bad habits and hurtful ways fits into a time to kill on God's great clock and readies us to move into a time for healing. Healing begins with forgiveness, and then recovery can begin.

There were a few sop drunks on Kelly's Creek who stayed on long toots. Two neighbors, Jack and Clyde, started drinking white likker one Friday afternoon. Soon, their sheets were in the wind and they decided to wobble down Greenwood Lane towards the town of Dillard. Neither of them could hit the ground with their hat.

Upon arriving at the train depot, a fight broke out that resulted in Clyde getting a fat lip. While retracing their path towards home, they decided to rest in the ditch line alongside the road. They were all propped up like kings on a throne in a reclining position with their feet sticking out of the ditch. Along came Mr. Dowdle on his way to buy seeds. He said, "Boys ain't you 'purdy'. How's that likker you're drinking?"

Jack said, "It must be th' best; Clyde has swelled

his lip hittin' the bottle too much."

Mr. Dowdle said, "Well folks, I gotta be movin' along. Ya'll watch across that field over there. Ray's mare is about to foal a brown, flop-eared mule. If you see it, try to catch it."

Not long after he left Jack spotted something brown with floppy ears moving in the brush and took off after a rabbit yelling, "Neigh! Neigh! Colt! Colt! Here's your mama you stupid mule!"

Jack swore off drinking for a spell after that embarrassing event and Clyde took some time off the bottle until his lips healed.

~ ~ ~

The meaning of the word "heal" in the Greek language is to mend by stitching and is a process that takes many forms. The wise proverb, "A stitch in time saves nine," is life-saving advice. Procrastination often hinders healing. Regardless, an appointed time to heal shall happen whether in this realm or the next. Modern doctors and nurses have the gift of healing accompanied with knowledge in medical practices. Appalachian culture has a long history of practicing folk medicine. Early mountaineers lived in isolation and depended on faith healers and midwives living in deep hollows over-shadowed by faith, tree limbs, and blue sky. They labored in love with prayers, herbs and other mixtures hoping to perfect cures as best they could to help ailing folks. Their practice has all but disappeared. Granny Lou kept a medicine shelf well stocked with whiskey, rock candy, honey, vinegar, iodine, turpentine, salt, soda, dried herbs and anything else she thought useful.

Among freehearted healers were those who could stop blood and cure thrash (thrush). One unusual practice was to talk the fire out of burns. They believed the burn would inflame the bone if not commanded to release itself from the victim into the universe. The practice was also called "blowing the fire out." I think faith healing worked because the strong faith of the healer was transfered to the patients, giving them hope of recovery.

Milk sickness was greatly feared in the mountains. It was associated with free-range cattle that ate white snakeroot and other poison plants. The poison was transferred through milk to calves and people. Many early Appalachians died from violent tremors and pain. Faith healers treated the afflicted with lots of sugar or starch believing it acted like a sponge to absorb the poison.

Mountain communities also had their own self-taught veterinarians to treat sick animals, especially cows and ewes in difficult deliveries.

Common sense goes a long way. Mountaineer Bob Justus told about a choking heifer:

"A whole apple lodged in her throat. While others stood around discussing what to do, Papa told a couple of men to hold the animal down with her neck across a thick board. He hit the board with a wooden maul smashing the apple. The heifer may have had a severe sore throat for a while but it lived to become a fine cow."

Another method used for choking was drenching the animal with mineral oil.

One of the most powerful tools of healing is words. The Bible says, *"A word fitly spoken is like apples of gold in pictures of silver."*—Proverbs 25:11

Jesus healed by speaking words. He never used the same method of healing twice, teaching us there is no set formula. He also used the power of touch. Positive healing energy flows when we embrace others.

Our two-year-old grandson Christopher often accompanies me on mountain paths. He becomes fearful of sections beyond his ability to master. His small dependent face shows unsureness until I extend a helping hand. The power of touch gives him needed courage to press on.

Chapter 4

A Time to Break Down, and A Time to build Up

Generally, it takes more time to build anything up than to break things down. I suppose that is one reason a time to break down can be difficult especially for old-timers like my brother, Ellis. Change threatens familiar scenes within his comfort zone. Sometimes, heavy rain causes Kelly's Creek to suddenly rise to flood stage washing away and breaking up his carefully groomed fields. A strong wind can easily lay a field of corn on the ground. Sometimes change to landscapes comes slowly like icicles melting in the sunshine.

A time to break down can also be positive with new challenges and opportunities to grow.

Ellis has seen many breakdowns and changes in our small community. "Well, th' biggest break down and change was when textile factories came here and lured people off th' farms. You can't blame people for easier jobs, but it cost us a lot of freedom. Until then, nobody worked on Sunday. Most people now live in the fast lane from the job to Walmart. I miss the closeness of communities. Cultivating the land changed, too. As far as I know, the first farm tractor to grace the Kelly's Creek community was brought here by Kelly Ritchie who was kinda an agriculture adviser feller'. It was an old Farmall brand. He'd sorta show it off plowing fields for neighbors, but some of the old timers like Uncle Frank Harkins wouldn't have it. He said the motor-plow skeered th' livestock and made too much racket.

"I'd not swap a good mule for a yard full of brand new tractors. A tractor don't know GEE and HAW and it packs th' ground too hard with heavy wheels and tires. Soil has t' be softened and fine before seed will take root downward and bear fruit upward.

"It grieved Uncle Frank, and it does me, t' look

over once productive patches and fields at weeds and thorns. I'll tell ye one thing though, it is hard plowin' in fallow ground.

"One time this feller' was makin' rounds in a field with his horse. When th' plowshare hooked a big rock, it nearly jerked his teeth out. Th' briars an' thorns hit him around his arms an' legs and he'd wipe blood an' cuss up a storm. Along come th' preacher an' said, 'You ought not cuss like that.' The feller' said, ' It's enough t' make a preacher cuss! Here, you try it a'round or two.' Sure enough, th' preacher ended his row with a few choice words of his own, It WILL make a' preacher cuss!

"Long ago, Uncle Frank said, Ellis, I'll not live to see it, but this place will be taken over with power lines, paved roads and metal gates. I'd rather the land go back to th' way it was when th' Indians were here."

Fallow ground brings to mind one of my favorite Bible verses from the great book of Jeremiah. *"Break up your fallow ground, and sow not among thornes."* —Jeremiah 4:3

Fallow ground becomes unproductive because of neglect. Weeds, thorns, and ugly briars scattered by the wind take root and eventually take over the entire area. A once productive and beautiful garden becomes a tangled mess.

Such was once the scene inside my heart. Poison seeds of man-made doctrines and religious bondage became deeply rooted. Sharp thorns of rituals, self-will, guilt, legalism, judgment, and other abominable weeds invaded my thinking and left no room for the discovery of true spiritual freedom--something I knew nothing about.

Reflecting back, I'm sure God tried to get my attention many times. Back in the 1970s, my high school journalism teacher, Eliot Wigginton, accompanied me and several other students to Berkeley, California, to speak at The National Commission of Resources for Youth to spread the glow of alternative education. On a break, we sat on a grassy spot across from a giant cathedral. It looked like a castle I'd seen in magazines. I marveled at its size. I greatly admired the artwork and huge stained glass windows. My teenage mind returned to the small churches scattered about in the Georgia mountains. They were no comparison to the site before me. I recall saying, "Wow, what a house for God!"

Wig's comment was forever engraved in my mind. "You think God lives over there? All they have is money."

At the time, according to my programmed, religious view, I thought his words blasphemous. I learned years later how true those words really were. God can't be contained in buildings or boxes.

Another wakeup call came in the form of a little child in 1999. I was attending a local church steeped in legalisms with endless lists of "dos and don'ts." I watched from a pew as a young mother guided her small sons to take a seat in front of me. Obviously, she told her boys they were going to God's house. Soon, a tall lanky elder, dressed in Sunday's best, began making his rounds shaking hands with the congregation. When he passed by the little tykes, one tugged on his sleek coattail, looking up in total awe. The little boy asked twice, "Mister, are you GOD? Mister are you GOD?" At that appointed moment, I knew I was no different from the child. I, too, did not know the difference between man's house and God's.

On the appointed day in the year 2010, symbolically the Master Plowman hooked a golden plow to a team of smashing white horses and drove it into the fallow ground of my heart. He guided and pulled silver reigns left and right, causing me to take serious personal inventory. The royal team made painful rounds, uprooting deep-seated beliefs from old cracked and dried religious systems. Slowly, hardened textures inside my heart changed to fine, fertile soil suitable for receiving seeds of freedom. All that could be shaken was shaken and ground to powder as the mighty towers of confusion fell. The crash was great, the smoke thick and the ashes deep. The entire experience was, in truth, like having an eggbeater inside my head. I experienced the true meaning of repentance. According to Strong's Exhaustive Concordance of the Bible, repentance means to change the way we think.

Playing church was broken down and ended for me in April, 2010. Now, I know the grand difference between religion and reality. Reality is Christ. My cathedral is in the mountains and the place where I am most built up.

"Stand fast therefore in the liberty wherewith Christ hath made us free, and be not entangled again with the yoke of bondage."
--Galatians 5:1

A Time for Every Purpose

~ ~ ~

It is impossible to build up when weighted down with outside forces and obstacles. Clean and firm foundations are a must.

This 175-year-old cabin stands in the Kelly's Creek community as a memorial to the heroes of my youth. It bears the stamp of the pioneer characters who built it. My ancestors shouldered large responsibilities and hardships that I will never know. Warm feelings ascend from the remains as voices of the past echo messages of commitment, respect, honesty, unity, trust, and faith.

We are strengthened when considering the ways of our forefathers and how they weathered seasonal storms and remained standing. We can't keep the pioneer ways, but we can build on their values.

Seeds of their examples ripen over time and fit together like the deeply notched logs.

~ ~ ~

Other than early influences of family, my second greatest character builder was at school. Many lifelong lessons are retained, especially those acquired in Eliot Wigginton's (Wig) Foxfire class in the mountains of north Georgia. It is hard to define the magical glow in his classroom emitted by both staff and students.

Wig wrote in his book, Sometimes a Shining Moment, "I knew in advance the mood I would have to project would be not, I know you come to me severely lacking in skills and my job is to fix your inadequacies, but rather, I know you can do good work in language arts and my job is to prove it to you, and have you prove it to yourselves. Before this class is over, you will be amazed at what you can create, I knew the mood in the classroom would largely have to be one of celebration, amazements, surprise, adventure--a series of constant unfolding experiences that would have them exclaiming to their peers over lunch about what they were doing. I wanted them coming into class every day ready for action." —Eliot Wigginton, "Sometimes A Shining Moment" (New York: Doubleday, 1995) ibid.,p.330.

Fellow student, Laurie and I became involved with Foxfire's activities about the same time in the 1970s. The experience was life changing for both of us. She said, "Wig was truly a teacher who stirred me to learn. In my personal experience, he never did that by telling me what to think or telling me what I had to do. I was sitting in the Foxfire office once, and as he passed by me, he threw some papers down and said, "What do you think about that?" It was not an assignment of any kind, it was something he had run across that had the seed of an idea in it. He let me spot that seed for myself and figure out how to grow it." Laurie is now a free-lance writer, and editor living in Virginia.

The Foxfire staff empowered young people with abilities, confidence, and courage simply because they believed students could preserve and share the knowledge of plain living before it disappeared.

Respect for contacts was paramount. They had survived for years self-sufficient. Regardless if we agreed or disagreed with our elder's opinions and beliefs, they received double honor. The older generation were very set in their ways. Contact Annie Perry told a male staff member to get a hair-cut or don't come back, and he did. Before the first interviews, students learned all the ropes needed to tie up an article. Using cassette recorders and expensive cameras made me nervous as we only had two and were on a tight budget.

A few Foxfire students spent a lot of time at the home of Garland and Hazel Willis, working on a personality sketch. They lived about an hour away from the office on Tellico Creek in Western North Carolina. Garland was an aging Missionary Baptist preacher with much advice to offer. "The Bible says, Forsake not the assembling of yourselves together. It makes little difference to assemble in a building if you don't first assemble yourself with God."

He frowned on worldly fashion like nail polish and make-up, and often spoke about Jezebel, a wicked queen in the Bible who painted her face before the dogs ate her. He admonished, "Stay away from Jezebel things, like painting your face and dancing. The Lord don't put a dancing foot and a praying knee on the same leg."

I wanted to ask him about King David dancing before the Lord, but dared not.

Mrs. Willis had the gift of hospitality and a full dining table. She had a pleasant countenance and was the picture of a pastor's wife. During interviews she sat in a straight chair near Garland and occasionally pushed back locks of gray hair from her shining face. She was silent during interviews but had plenty to say off the tape. "I married Garland after his first wife died, and I was quite young. I knew nothing about man and wife stuff. In fact, I married a preacher because I surely thought they didn't do such. Lord, was I wrong! After Garland convinced me it was all right, I nearly bled t' death. No wonder I didn't care for it." After that, we Foxfire kids didn't know whether to spit or go blind, so we all laughed.

Other Foxfire activity involved recording mountain superstitions, folk tales, ghost stories, recipes, remedies, instructions for building things, hunting tales and mountain philosophy that was collected and filed. Information flowed like pouring water downhill.

My neighbor, Eldon Miller was an avid hunter. He agreed to let us document a wild boar hunt. He loosed his dogs from chains and they began frantically sniffing the ground. Soon the pack raged and rousted up a big wild boar roaming in a waist high brown sage field. I was taking pictures midway between a fence and a tree. Suddenly, like a streak of lightning, the boar flew right by me and disappeared into a thicket of ivy bushes. The dogs followed swiftly behind and the race was on. As the dogs charged past me, I went up that tree, dropping the camera on the ground.

From my elevated point, I could see raised bristles on three mountain curs that Mr. Eldon used as bay dogs. They cornered the boar, and then kept their distance from it, waiting on a bulldog to rush in to catch and hold the boar. It came up from the rear to join the fight as if it had no fear and no brakes. The angry boar slung dogs in the air like rag dolls stuck on a ceiling fan. The dogs tumbled through the thickets, yelped, then returned to the fight.

Finally, the bulldog laid hold on the boar. Blood curdling squeals and sounds of a vicious fight made me glad to be up a tree. I felt sorry for the hog as it put up a good fight. Mr. Eldon bravely ran up the hill to his dogs. He choked the bulldog to make it turn loose. The boar was set free, the dogs tied up and I came down from the tree thinking about how the article would take shape.

It was common to work on several articles at once. Well digging, dowsing for water with a forked stick, washing clothes in an iron pot, collecting recipes, as well as many personality sketches, were among my tasks.

Once the interviews were over, I worked long hours after school and at home transcribing the tapes in long hand. My folks enjoyed listening to the "talk box" by the firelight. Mounds of text grew for editing. I cut the text with scissors then taped it together, forming long rows on the floor. It was like working a puzzle to make the information fit smoothly together. Mama said, "How can anybody read such a mess?" I rolled the article up like a piece of carpet, and delivered it to typist, Margie Bennett. She was constantly pecking away on an old, black IBM typewriter making camera-ready copies suitable for gluing to graph paper for the final lay-outs.

I'd never been inside the tiny darkroom, afforded by a grant, located in The Foxfire office. It was so small, you couldn't cuss a cat without getting hair in your mouth. I quickly learned the purpose of the small red bulb overhead. It protected printing papers from getting light struck. The enlarger was fascinating to work with. It sorta looked and worked like a big microscope. Once the image was brought into focus and perfected, it was burned onto photo paper. Carefully, I learned how to transfer it into a pan of chemicals. Like magic, the pictures I'd taken appeared before my eyes.

The process continued to rinsing and drying on a heated chrome wheel. When the pictures were ready to incorporate in the article text on graph paper, final layouts began. The office smelled like the rubber cement we used to glue the text in place. It oozed around the edges and dried on the graph paper. We used our fingers to rub and clean away excess cement from the graph paper. It resembled peeling skin. The tile floors turned into a winter wonderland covered with bits of paper trimmings.

After many hours of preparation, the staff inspected the final work. Once approved, a few students took the magazine to the printing company in Atlanta.

A Time for Every Purpose

In my feeble efforts to write today, I still use the old method before transferring it to a computer file.

Many students were placed in unimaginable situations and unfamiliar territories. I, along with staff member Laurie and a few other students were stranded in Harlan, KY, enroute to Alice Lloyd College during gasoline rationing in 1973.

I stood outside our motel room wondering if we'd ever make it home as I watched cars laden with black coal dust pass by, thinking a car wash would be a gold mine up here!

Probably the most challenging and memorable experience for all who worked on the article was entering a snake handling church. Fellow students David, Karen, and Gary were invited and given free rein to document the services--an opportunity open to very few journalists. Foxfire's involvement with the small congregation lasted nine months until enough information was gathered to honestly portray the people who used their freedom of religion.

Can you imagine swinging a camera around into the face of a giant rattlesnake, or being offered to hold one during the very energetic service? Not only were snakes passed around like coffee in a saucer, several lamps filled with kerosene were lit. During the intensity of the service, several members held the flames to their bare feet or ran it through their hair without harm. *The People Who Take Up Serpents* is included in the Foxfire 7 book.

The experiences are countless. Andrea and Laurie navigated New York City. Doug experienced other cultures in Kodiak, Alaska. I cringed at public speaking and reading aloud, yet because of Foxfire's strong character building I stood before a packed audience at The Washington Hilton addressing The National Trust for Historic Preservation meeting. They were interested in involving other students in similar programs.

Looking back, I now see that Foxfire's mentors built on the same foundations used in our culture. Just as Appalachian communities gathered together to build a cabin, raise a barn, harvest crops, make a casket or just support each other, so did the Foxfire students combine efforts. We grew in character and commitment together.

There is a series of twelve books, with over nine-million in print.

Chapter 5

A Time to Weep, and A Time to Laugh

How could we know the joy of laughter without the sadness of weeping? Times of weeping are like thick dark clouds filled with heavy rain in our heart. If we could not weep to release inside pressure, our brains might explode like a jitter pot (pressure cooker) of beans on the ceiling. Tears are heaven's natural irrigation watering the soul and helps wash away grief and pain. We all pass through valleys of sorrow and weeping. Yet, there are streams of blessings in valleys.

I suppose more tears are shed at funerals and gravesides than any other time. Entire mountain communities weep together when a loss of life occurs. Long ago, the slow tolling of the church bell announced a death. The number of tolls revealed the age of the deceased. People working in the fields or in hearing distance knew who it was. The ringing of the church bell is uncommon now, but I last heard the tolling of the church bell in June, 2012. Seventy-five tolls chilled the air announcing the passing of a friend and neighbor, Bill Kelly.

In early Appalachian communities, friends laid all things aside to gather selflessly and freely with grieving mountain families to offer comfort and support. Bed linens were stripped from the deathbed to cover a board on which the body was washed and dressed. Time was of essence before rigor mortis began. Skilled carpenters crafted a simple coffin then padded it with cotton. The cotton was covered with white or black fabric. That night, twenty or thirty neighbors sat up with the dead. Sometimes they sang soft hymns or recalled events and memories of the deceased.

Wooden coffin in an old time church. Photo courtesy of Foxfire.

The grave was prepared by neighbors, also, who gathered in the cemetery with shovels, mattocks and picks to dig a six-foot deep hole. They felt it was the last thing they could do for the deceased. The Scaly Mountain community, just up the hill from our house, still digs graves by hand. A crowd shows up at the cemetery, most of which are young people, so it is likely the tradition will continue for many years.

The next day the coffin was loaded in a horse drawn wagon, and then taken to the church for the funeral. Sad singing and slow walking to the gravesite followed. Neighbors lowered the deceased into the ground then covered the coffin with dirt. Afterwards, folks returned to the home to clean with lye soap and disinfect by scalding everything possible. During seasons of weeping it is impossible to laugh, but in time laughter returns.

I guess we have all been tickled like a hen caught on an electric fence. There is a lot of truth in the saying, "We laughed 'till we cried" and, "You might as well laugh as t' cry for th' good it does." The same hormones, leucine, and encephalin, are released during uncontrollable outbursts of both laughter and weeping.

It's December 29 as I write this piece and the birthday of Foxfire's beloved contact, Aunt Arie Carpenter. Her character was one of uncommon love and decency, felt by all who met her. Most of her ninety-two years were spent helping others. She took life, hard as it came, with a chuckle saying, "Ah, well, this world and one more and a turnip patch'll do us all."

I recall she loved to laugh, and we loved to laugh with her. Laughter was her medicine. She said, "I don't reckon th' Devil'll get me fer laughin', but if he does, he'll shore get me 'cause I've always done more'n'my share a'th' laughin' in th' world."

Perhaps due to isolation, mountain people like my father-in-law William Woodall created their own humor as a means of entertainment.

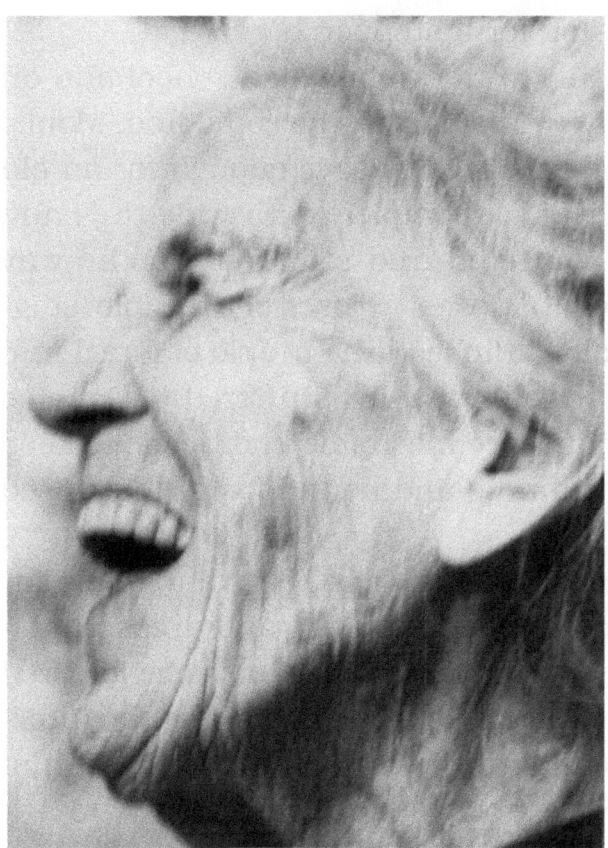

Aunt Arie
Used with permission from Foxfire
www.foxfire.org

My much younger brother-in-law, Douglas, is an overcomer on many levels. He graduated high school in 1985.

The mountains offered slim chances for employment beyond odd jobs with low wages. He was not content to accept limited means of living for his talents. Fueled by determination and courage, he set his sights on Georgia Institute of Technology (Georgia Tech), located in Atlanta. It was a high goal for any mountain kid, but Douglas was no stranger to obstacles. It was "no step for a stepper."

Douglas began to work after high school and on weekends at whatever menial jobs he could find. Money was scarce but he managed to save enough for an old blue Ford pick-up truck complete with wide tires and sporty rims. It sputtered and stuttered on the way home, so he named it "Moses." Moses of the Bible staggered at the call of God to lead the people of Israel into the promised land because he stuttered. Douglas gained enough shade tree mechanic knowledge to keep stuttering Moses running and bound for the promised land of college.

He swapped his dusty work boots and jeans for shiny leather shoes, collared shirts, and dress pants. He climbed in Moses and left mountain solace for tired roads of asphalt where people rushed along the interstates wearing headphones, and some drove past him reading books. Sights and sounds of a big city to Appalachian people can feel like cultural shock.

Douglas quickly made new friends at college who were eager to visit his mountains.

On one occasion, he and several friends were snowed in at our home on Kelly's Creek. After a hearty mountain breakfast, Georgia Tech student Carl rubbed his full belly, then took a morning shower. He emerged with his hair sticking straight up as if he had seen a haint in the bathroom. Larry (my husband) remarked, "Lord have mercy! WHAT happened to your hair?"

Carl replied, "I put mousse in it."

Larry said, "Well, hell far' I've heard of having your butt on your shoulders, but never moose in your hair. That's a new one on me!"

We laughed and played cards while the snow slowly melted, revealing passable roads to release Douglas and his friends from mountain care.

One weekend in April, an aspiring Douglas returned home from college. After taking a deep breath of Bogg's Mountain clean air and unloading dirty laundry and a stack of books and pencils, his tall lanky body strolled through an overgrown field searching for the distant voices of his family who was digging out a new vein of spring water below the house.

Douglas's dad, a skilled dowser had found the underground spring water using a green "V" shaped forked stick. He held it in place by his teeth and thumb to prevent hand interference as the stick moved back and forth over the unseen water during the divining process. Several passes over the water's path pinpointed where to dig.

He knew his Bible and said the children of Israel used dowsing long ago. Numbers, chapter 21 tells of one account. Verse 18 states, *"The nobles of the people digged it (a well), by the direction of the lawgiver (Moses), with their staves."* Sure enough, the word staves in Hebrew means a stick. Scientists cannot explain how it works, and colleges don't know much about the practice that is sometimes called "water witching."

Sounds of picks and shovels, grumbles and moans directed Douglas to the site. He turned his educated attention to the red ditch line where we were digging. The sight of wet, mud-covered clothing was not uncommon to him as he thought of an easier way to pool up the drinking water. Douglas stood quietly observing the task. His dad jokingly said, "Step back folks, this college feller has come to dig this out with his pencil!"

Douglas blushed then joined us in laughter. He graduated from Georgia Tech and became Vice President of a local bank. He built a new house on the Woodall homestead and enjoys that same sweet spring water today.

Mr. Woodall like many mountain folks saw humor in just about everything, "If there ain't no fools, there ain't no fun."

Once he invited me to cross the yard and see the family truck. Soon an old, paint-flaked International pickup came into view. I asked, "Why do you call it the family truck?"

He replied, "Because it takes the whole family to push it!"

When asked how many children they had, he replied, "Four living and two married."

Chapter 6

A Time to Mourn, and A Time to Dance

There is an appointed time to experience deep grief during our journey in the flesh. Mourning is a natural response when loss occurs. Jesus promised in the beatitudes, *"Blessed are they who mourn for they shall be comforted."*—Matthew 5:4

My in-laws, William and Clara Woodall reared their family in the south end of the county on Boggs mountain.

They owned and operated a sawmill business near their home. The hum of a huge saw blade moving back and forth cutting logs into lumber along with the tinkling of a dust doodler chain directed visitors to the work area, where fresh sawdust scents filled the air.

Mr. Woodall was tall and handsome. Clear blue eyes sparkled underneath a dusty cap that shadowed a shy face, and a pleasant smile. He referred to himself as "Raggedy Bill" when dressed in worn, somewhat baggy green work britches he adjusted often by twisting the waistline. I guess it was a focus aid when matters required his undivided attention. He was also a proud Army veteran of WWll, but rarely spoke of war experiences.

His daughter Glenda held a special place in his heart, being their first-born girl. She finished high school, moved to another county to take a job, and later married David Jackson. It was a bittersweet change, especially for Mr.Woodall. In time, Glenda and David had a beautiful baby boy. The Woodalls were thrilled, and Little David became the central focus at family gatherings for seventeen months.

On a gloomy November day, a patrol car pulled up into the Woodall's yard to deliver devastating news. A deputy said, "I'm sorry to be the bearer of bad news, but there has been an accident. Little David has drowned."

Details were few and unimportant at that time. Mr. Woodall habitually adjusted his britches and sank down on his piano bench. The air became chilled like early winter with the unexpected grief. Reality sank in, shattering our hearts like hot marbles dropped in an ice bucket. My sister-in-law, Debra, and I went to break the sad news to other family members.

When I arrived at the funeral home, Glenda was

bending low over Little David's lifeless body. She could not loose herself from his side; in fact, she was numb to the presence of others. Her blouse was wet from a river of tears as she intensely held his tiny cold hands with a continual expression of her deep love and grief. There are no comforting words for mourning like that.

Friends gathered at Camp Creek Baptist Church and watched as the undertaker slowly unloaded the heaviest little box in the universe. Inside, the congregation arose from the hardest of seats in respect as the family passed down a narrow aisle towards the front of the church. An old upright piano played ever so softly:

You are my sunshine, my only sunshine
You make me happy, when skies are gray
You'll never know, dear how much I love you
Please don't take my sunshine away
The other night, dear when I lay sleeping
I dreamed I held you in my arms
When I awoke dear, I was mistaken
And I hung my head and cried

Mr. Woodall sat near a window with his silver head bowed low, holding his cap in his hand. Crystal tears leaked from his soft blue eyes that he wiped with the back of his rough sawmill hands. The preacher spoke words no one heard, for none could penetrate the thick veil of deep mourning. Our sunshine had been taken away. The stars fell from the sky, the moon ceased to give light for a long time. It has been said that time heals all wounds, but in reality, time only puts distance between mourning and pain. Later,

A Time for Every Purpose

Glenda told me that in her darkest hours, she held a lock of Little David's first haircut next to her heart. It was the smallest part of him, but better than nothing.

Years later, Glenda and David had a baby girl, never to replace Little David, but another ray of sunshine they could hold and love.

Wise Solomon said it is better to go to the house of mourning than to a party, because funerals and mourning cause us to think about what is important. I believe to find comfort during seasons of mourning, one must be able to look beyond present circumstances into a much brighter future.

Entertainment was slim around our place until

Mama sold enough butter and buttermilk to buy a record player from Jower's Appliance store in nearby Clayton. Dad loaded it into the back of his pick-up truck, tied it down with a rope, then headed for Kelly's Creek. Mama proudly placed it in the living room under a shelf stacked with a few 45-RPM records. After supper on Saturday night, she would start playing a song by Grandpa Jones, called *"Here Rattler, Here"* to get things jumping.

Old Rattler was a good old dog; As blind as he could be.
Ev'ry night 'bout supper time I believe that dog could see.

Here! Rattler, Here! Here!; Here! Rattler! Here!
Call old Rattler from the barn; Here! Rattler! Here!

Old Rattler tree'd the other night and
I thought he'd tree'd a coon.
When I come to find out he was barkin' at the moon.

Well, grandma had a yeller hen we set her as you know.
We set her on three buzzard eggs
and hatched out one old crow.

Grandpa had a muley cow she was muley when she's born.
It took a jaybird forty years to fly from horn to horn.

Now if I had a needle and thread as fine as I could sew,
I'd sew my sweetheart to my back;
And down the road I'd go.
Old Rattler was a smart old dog, even tho' he was blind
He wouldn't hurt one single thing,
even tho' he was very fine.

A Time for Every Purpose

*One night I saw a big fat coon climb up in a tree.
I called old Rattler right away to get 'im down fer' me.*

*But Rattler wouldn't do it because he liked that coon.
I saw them walkin' paw in paw later
by the light of the moon.*

*Now old Rattler's dead and gone like all good dogs do.
You better not act a dog yourself or you'll be goin' there, too.*

After the *Old Rattler* warmed us up, we were ready to tear the floor up buck-dancing (clogging) to other songs like, *"Down Yonder,"* by Doc Watson and other records by Bill Monroe. The music mixed with rhythmed feet sounded like the house was coming down. It made livers quiver.

The next day, Granny Lou placed her hands on a thin waistline above her tattered apron and commented, "If I wanted to hear that plumb up to my house, I'd buy myself a record player."

Brother Ellis afixed taps on his dancing shoes he wore at the Mountain City Playhouse just south of our home. It was a big building operated by the American Legion to raise needful funds. Admission cost fifty cents. It was a very popular spot for local people and tourists to gather for clean fun. It hosted small indoor circus acts and 'rasslin matches. During a 'rasslin event Paul Anderson, the world's strongest man, came from his hometown, Toccoa, Georgia.

Ellis remembers well meeting him. "Paul was raisin' funds t' build a youth home in Vidalia. He had a passion fer th' young folks. He tag teamed with professional 'rassler Johnny Weaver against th' Dalton brothers. Paul had whipped a Russian for an Olympic medal and said he didn't want t' know how much weight was added on him at th' Olympics cuz it was a mental thing. I think he lifted well over six thousand pounds with his back.

" Well, anyway, at The Mountain City Playhouse they had two swings mounted on poles. Four 'r five of th' county's heaviest men came to set in th' swings. Paul lifted them like feathers. Then he crawled under th' 'rasslin ring and lifted it into th' air. He put on a good show. He was th' type of man you don't ever forget meeting."

Chiefly, folks looked forward each week to square dances. The caller stood above the crowd with instructions. "Georgia a rang tang, do-si-do, right hand over the bird cage; bird high, swing four, hands across, shoot the star, four leaf clover, right hand swing, laid around."

The young danced with the old for an evening of exercise and fun. The dance ended about midnight. The memories still dance around and will never be cast away by those who experienced The Mountain City Playhouse.

Chapter 7

A Time to Cast Away Stones, and A Time to Gather Stones Together

There is an appointed time to cast away the heavy stones of division. Hatred, judgments, stereotypes, and prejudice are just a few things that rob us of peace and prevent union and growth.

Until my first book, *It's Not My Mountain Anymore*, was published, I rarely ventured southward beyond my county lines. One of the most memorable trips was through south Georgia en-route to the great state of Florida. As my friend, Becky Justus, and I pressed southwards, I noticed a white substance lining the roadside of long two-lane highways. It reminded me of Georgia mountain snow, but it was scattered cotton from massive white fields.

Becky pulled the car over for a closer look. I took my first step into the soft, sandy soil. It felt strange to mountain feet accustomed to rough texture. Looking out over the fields, my mind went back to a time in American history as the stains of slavery rushed in.

I envisioned the field alive and echoing with the songs of slaves dragging filled sacks of cotton.

I recalled reading about slavery in my own county in Dr. Andrew Ritchie's book, "Sketches of Rabun County History." He wrote that sixty families here owned slaves in 1862. Of the 248 slaves, the majority were women and children. Dr. Ritchie wrote, "I have personally known some of the men who had the most slaves and also some of the slaves themselves. I never got the idea that slaves were cruelly treated or that slavery was a brutal institution in this county. Slaves were kindly treated and well cared for."

Kind treatment is part of Appalachian character, yet it was not so in other areas of the country where slavery was a part of our cruel country's history.

As I stood in the massive cotton field, my eyes followed the long, straight rows to a green line of pine trees at its end. I imagined years of gross atrocities committed against young and old like homicide, rape, and unspeakable terrorism. The cotton bolls became stained with black blood as I envisioned a cruel master riding a horse carrying a whip as he quoted from a book: "The servant who knows the master's will and does not do what the master wants will be beaten with many stripes."

A very small structure resembling a slave cabin stood at the side of the field. I watched a few bees circling overhead threatening cruel stings before they landed on the old gray boards. Dodging the bees, I placed my hands on the waist high porch, pausing and reflecting. I could almost hear voices of lamentation coming from inside. It took five bloody years of

A Time for Every Purpose

Civil War to cast away the heavy stone of slavery, yet the heavy rocks bear down hard in American history.

In the distance, a hot sunset melted the western sky and spoke of the blazing days of toil. The same sun was a token of fading hopes of freedom for those who worked this land. I was standing on land once watered with tears as a people prayed for a better way of life. I wanted to pick some cotton to daub the hole in my heart.

Two-hundred years of slavery stains remain on Old Glory and are larger than all others combined as our country gathers stones of healing together. I recalled former President George Bush's words during African American history month: "We cannot carry the message of freedom and the baggage of bigotry at the same time. We have made progress and our work is not yet done, but we can proceed with faith in our country and confidence in our cause"

Slave-cabin: Sautee-Nacoochee Center- http://www.snca.org/)
This 1850s slave cabin was still standing on the property of Jim Johnston who generously donated the cabin to the Sautee Nacoochee Center near Helen, GA for historical preservation.

Gathering lots of stones is part of life in the mountains of southern Appalachia. During spring and summer, gathering stones is a daily activity in gardens and fields. Mama said, "You can pile rocks all day, then after the dew rises, they beat you back to the field. I do declare, you can pick up one and two will grow in its place."

Each turn of the plow unearths more and more rocks. Like those who came before us, we continue to pile the gathered rocks along the banks of the creek. Once a hindrance and a nuisance, those gathered stones serve the purpose of keeping the waters of the creek within their banks.

When we changed Grandpa Taylor's headstone, I brought the old one home and set it up in a field near a huge rock.

One day young Sterling inquired about the old headstone. I took a deep breath and said, "Well, grandson, it's like this:

A feller passed through here who wouldn't behave, so he got a rock thrown on top of him. Can you take a lesson?"

Sterling pondered my answer with piercing eyes, then started laughing. "Nanny, you can't pick up that big rock!"

~ ~ ~

Amy Ammons Garza and Doreyl Ammons Cain are strong pillars among us who deeply value our heritage. I became acquainted with Amy through a mutual friend when I was about to publish my first book. After a few moments in her presence, our spirits were connected in a common cause, Appalachian heritage.

"My sister Doreyl, brother David and I grew up in an old wooden house in a cove alongside Grassy Creek Road in the Tuckasegee Valley located in Jackson County, North Carolina. The house had only three rooms. A living room that held a potbellied stove with benches in the back where we young'uns sat in the wintertime, a small table with a battery-operated radio, a couple of chairs, and an old organ. The one and only bedroom had two beds—all three of us young'uns slept in one of them, and our parents slept in the other.

"Tuckasegee Valley was in almost complete isolation from the rest of the world. We had no inside plumbing, no electricity, and, all summer long, no shoes. We carried water in buckets from the spring above the house, our only light came from kerosene oil lamps with smoky glass chimneys, and our school clothes were made by Mother's hands from feed-sack material.

"A large wooden table covered by oilcloth almost filled our kitchen with long benches on either side. Along the far wall stood a wood-burning cook stove and a wood box. Shelves covered the walls holding our dishes, a small amount of cooking supplies and utensils. The linoleum-covered floor had been scrubbed so many times by our dirt-conscious Mother that it had lost its luster and had worn down so it had holes in it corresponding to the slats in the floor. Many's the time I saw my brother slip cornbread through the cracks in the floor to feed our dog, Smoky, underneath.
Our glass-canned goods were stored outside in the canhouse. The canhouse actually had two floors. It was the second floor that housed three creative minds that were destined to record the history of our ancestors. That was the playroom where we three spent long hours instilling the world we lived in into our memory.

"The canhouse was a diverse world; for example, the first floor of the canhouse was filled with vegetables and fruit in the process of drying. It became our church where we held our own revivals.

A Time for Every Purpose

David would preach at our pretend pulpit while Doreyl and I sang out of our songbook (the Sears and Roebuck catalog). David pounded and yelled that we were all going to hell if we didn't quit our sinning ways, Doreyl and I held up the "Amen" corner quite well.

"Along the sides of the walls, the three of us had collected old kitchen utensils that became our musical instruments that were beat upon, scrapped upon and pounded upon.

"Just imagine, there in a quiet cove on Grassey Creek Road, with no noise other than nature for miles, all of a sudden the sounds of many spoons, sticks, tin cups hitting pots and pans, the scrapping of thimbles on a washboard, and dried beans beating against a mason jar. Smoky the dog sang many a featured song to the tune of 'dishpan valley' by our 'canhouse band.

"In the front yard grew the largest black walnut tree I had ever seen, and tied to the limb near the middle was a rope. At the other end of the rope, near the ground, was an old tire on which I used to swing far out over the creek...and back again. Each time I would swing out, my legs would pump the tire higher so I could reach the leaves of the walnut with my feet. I would make believe I was touching the tallest tree at the top of the tallest mountain that seemed to touch the sky all around our little cove.

"I was but a teenager when Daddy took a job in South Carolina and we left the mountains. Life's struggles slapped me in the face, stealing the innocence and creativity of childhood, the freedom of choice, the sense of belonging. As Doreyl, David, and I grew into adulthood, like birds, we flew away from home. I ,the eldest, wound up in Northwest Indiana with a husband and a truck and trailer repair shop, and raising two daughters. Doreyl, my sister, married and had her own art design company in California, where she was bringing up two boys. David married and he and his wife became teachers in the South Carolina school system. Constantly, we were on the phone, talking to each other, always longing to be together, feeling the call of the mountains.

"Once you're caught in the web of adulthood, necessities of the world you've built around you take over. The needs of those you've grown to love and to support come first. And all the while the road back grows longer and more rocky. Caught in this trap, it is very difficult to all of a sudden decide that maybe the real reason the joy has gone out of your soul is you're in the wrong place. You're not flowering in the cement of modern society.

"As I developed into an author, I also started doing storytelling at the local libraries in Indiana, where people would come to listen. I think partially to hear my mountain accent. The stories all about growing up in the mountains, and with every story I told, the homesickness grew worse.

"Once or twice a year I drove eight-hundred miles round trip back home to get filled up with the Blue Ridge Mountains. I never quit dreaming of coming home to stay.

"During my visits to the mountains, something strange happened. There had been emptiness in my soul that I had not even realized. A sense of belonging began to cover me like a warm hand-stitched quilt. It seemed as though I could see my Grandpa walking beside me, his cane tapping the rocky road. At times, Grandma would show up swishing through the gooseberry bushes ahead of me, her voice encircling my head with wise sayings. The cool earth beneath my feet took me back to planting seeds in the ground, walking behind Daddy as he plowed the fields calling out to the mule 'Gee...Haw.' And in the evening hours, I could hear my mother telling me to haul the bucket of spring water in to fill the kettle on the wood stove so we could take a bath before dark.

"Back in Indiana, I craved the mountains. I could not stand it any longer and had to do something about it.

"The words came out of the sky, 'It's time!' They were loud in my ears, settling deep into my heart. Sitting on the porch steps gazing at an August blue moon, I knew what the words meant. There was no question, only acceptance, yet they frightened me beyond measure. I immediately realized the weight of the responsibility and how it would change my life forever.

"One night, as I talked on the phone to my sister in California, I told her of my dream. Lo and behold, she said she had been dreaming of doing the same thing. In the evenings, she had been illustrating spontaneous drawings at events there in California, and as she drew, it had drawn her near to the time when we were kids, when she had listened to the birds in the trees and began to draw them in the dirt because Daddy could not afford to buy her paper and pencils. I recorded that memory with a poem.

She'd have with her a stick broken from a tree
She'd look all around until the right place she'd see
Then down on her knees in the dirt road she'd go
Blond curls shining, head bent low
And leaning forward she'd stretch out her hand
To smooth and smooth and pat the sand
Then, pausing a moment, her hands on her skirt
She'd take her stick and right there in the dirt
In a wink, a flutter, all in plain sight
A cardinal! A sparrow! Wings in flight!
With her strokes the birds awoke and flew
With her laugher, my heart, so full flew too
And above her, among the limbs of the trees
Eyes of all nature, animals, birds and bees
Watched in wonderment as this girl child drew
And drew and drew and drew and drew
Time lost! abandoned! Time standing still
Creation came flying over stream and hill
There on the mountain, knees on the ground
The swisssh of the wind the only sound
With just a stick, a laugh, a magical hand
A miracle took place right there in the sand
For her gift erupted and rose on high
To fly forever, winging, winging in the sky.

"Doreyl, David and I were so far apart. I looked over my shoulder through the screen door to the image of my husband as he sat reading in his easy chair. Emotion welled and as the breeze touched my cheeks, I felt the wetness of the tears. I'll have to leave him, I thought, and then began to cry in earnest.

"Phil and I had been married only five years, and

just six months before he had been diagnosed with Leukemia. Now in remission, his heath had improved, along with his work schedule. Although retired from the trucking business, his whole professional life revolved around his Chicago trucking magazine and his writing. He would never drop this 'purpose for his life,' and I would never ask him to do that for my benefit. So, I sat there on the porch step and quietly cried.

"For the next week I continued trying to hide my despair from Phil, not knowing how to tell him what had happened. I slipped even deeper into depression. But not once did I think I should ignore what I had heard; there was no question about it. I knew beyond all reasoning's that I had to return to my homeland and work with the mountain children. I had a message for them.

"After a week of wrestling with the whole of this change in my life, I finally knew I had to tell this man I loved so deeply what I had to do.

"Phil," I said that evening, "I have to tell you something. Come sit with me on the couch."

"As he sat down, I took his hand and quietly told him what I had experienced. He was silent a moment, then he smiled at me. "Why…is that all?" he said. "With all the crying, I was worried you wanted to leave me for good!" He put his arms around me, hugging me close.

"The Lord has trusted you with a calling, Amy!" he said. "That's all there is to it. I'll help you with all I have! And, just know, Amy…if you've been called to do the Lord's bidding, whatever you need will be provided for you at the right time."

"I gazed at this husband of mine! Once more there was his validation, support and encouragement to our Lord, to our partnership, and to me.

"Phil did as he promised, supporting me as I set out on my journey going home to North Carolina, and finding a place to live. Every month I would travel to northwest Indiana and stay a week with Phil--seven hundred fifty-four miles right to the doorstep--I drove it in one day. How we treasured those days we spent together!

"And so, twenty-six years ago, although Doreyl and I were separated by more than 2000 miles, over the phone wires, the Ammons Sisters performance team was born. We came home with a full purpose, to conduct creative writing and visual art workshops in the schools, and found that the children were receptive to the stories we told of growing up in the mountains. We'd been away for so long, and it was obvious that our heritage was eroding. Something must be done or all the stories we'd been told as children would be lost forever. We wanted to give back to our community. Doreyl and I founded Catch the Spirit of Appalachia, a nonprofit organization, out of which grew a dedicated board of directors who worked alongside us to accomplish our work in the community festivals, youth mountain talent contests, teaching art and writing, publishing local writers, providing scholarships to young Appalachians, and producing a radio program called *Stories of Mountain Folk*.

"During our performances we share with the children and invite them down to the stage to join us, and once again, along with the thump of our canhouse band. Doreyl and I re-live our childhood. My heart fills every time I dance with a child and watch young eyes light up and smiles play like spring rain on the faces in the audience.

"I feel so rich. I would not trade it for all the diamonds and rubies in the world. It's our precious heritage."

Today, in classrooms, before a general audience, or during area festivals, you can find Amy, Doreyl and David, dressed in the traditional clothing, celebrating their mountain heritage and representing Catch the Spirit of Appalachia.

Doreyl, spontaneous artist, and Amy, storyteller, at a school assembly

Catch the Spirit of Appalachia's tireless work is a precious gift for future generations to build upon. I'm honored to be a small pebble gathered in their collection of heritage stones. (You can check out their work at spiritofappalachia.com; CSAbooks.com; or storiesofmountainfolk.com)

David Ammons, caning a chair at a festival.

Chapter 8

A Time to Embrace, and A Time to Refrain from Embracing

The secret to living the good life is learning to be content in all things, embracing both blessings and challenges, even when we cannot know in advance the outcome.

Good memories are worth embracing and create warmth around us that draws us closer to precious times of the past with family, friends and creation. As long as memories stay locked inside our heart, there is no end. Tomorrow is a gift of another opportunity to embrace others by a show of emotional support and to embrace our own strengths and weaknesses.

We have three grandchildren Sterling, Christopher, and Riley. I recall how Mama first embraced small children by pinching both cheeks saying, "That's what you do when words ain't enough." Then, she would hug them as only a grandmother can.

I recall a special time when I embraced young Sterling after a scary incident.

Sterling Cove Road runs up the right side of our property and is named for the eldest grandson. It is steeper than a horse's face. In fact, you can skin your nose walking up. When the county made official 911 maps, a shiny new sign was erected at the road's entrance. I told Sterling, "It's an honor to have a road named after you."

He wasn't impressed saying, "I'm not Sterling Cove, I'm STERLING DARNELL!"

In the winter, it seems we live just under the North Pole high in the mountains. Snowfall will lie on northern slopes until the spring thaw. The bottom of

A Time for Every Purpose

Sterling Cove road was clear and dry when Sterling and I hopped into "Casper," our trusty van, to scale the steep road to check water lines. I shifted Casper into granny gear and floor-boarded the gas pedal. We hit ice near the top and stalled between a bluff and a red clay bank.

Quickly, I unloaded Sterling telling him to stand in a safe place near a tree above the van while I shoveled dirt underneath the back tires from the bank. All seemed well. Sterling left his safe spot to come closer to the action near of the rear of the van.

Suddenly the van creaked and started sliding backwards. My heart skipped a beat. I dropped the shovel and lunged for a streak of blonde hair behind the moving van. Somehow, I grabbed him and threw him to safety on the bank. I was amazed how fast I moved that day and credit his save to supernatural intervention.

"Stay!" I commanded and nervously returned to rescue the van. The driver side door was open as I continued to add more dirt under the tires.

Again, the van slid backwards. I just knew it would be a total loss and wind up in the creek. I could hear Mama jest, "I guess it was thirsty and needed a drink."

The van continued to slide as the dirt under the tires turned to slick mud. Quickly, I jumped under the steering wheel, nervously guiding it backwards down Sterling Cove. Walking back up the road to get Sterling, I felt like death's playmate. I shuddered at the events that had just occurred. He jumped off the bank into my arms and we embraced tightly, giving thanks for a divine rescue. The scripture in Isaiah 65:24 was quickened in my mind: *"Before you call I will answer."* We sure were glad.

~ ~ ~

Sometimes situations arise that require us to refrain from embracing. Wise Solomon said, *"Withdraw thy foot from the neighbor's house: lest he be weary of thee..."* which means a 'body can wear out a welcome.

Mama usually followed his words with her own, "I like comers and goers, but darn comers and stayers. Havin' company will wear ye out worse than working."

Bedding was limited and simple. A common jest was, "Just come on, we're short on beds, but we'll hang you up on a nail." Guests got the best bed in the house.

Early Appalachian beds were made from straw or other natural materials. Some folks raised ducks to use their feathers in pillows and ticks. Once sheetings were sewed together forming ticks, they were filled with soft stuffings and laid on a rope bed that is similar to today's hammocks. Stuffing materials were changed often. Naturally, the best of housekeepers couldn't see tiny bugs gathered along with natural stuffing.

Living distance between family and friends generally required extended stays with mountain host families, who are very accommodating and strive to get along with the devil himself. They went an extra mile to avoid offending anyone, but when the time for embracing was over, hints were given that it was time for company to leave.

A Time for Every Purpose

"Sleep tight, don't let the bedbugs bite," is a term that some believe originated in Appalachia. Old fashioned rope beds had ropes webbing in the bed frame that was tightened with a wooden T-Handle to remove the sag, hence the reminder to "sleep tight."

Rope bed used with permission Foxfire www.foxfire.org

The first hint used by early Appalachians for guests to vacate was to loosen the bed ropes allowing the tick to sag and slip closer to the floor. If that didn't work, they would serve a cold shoulder of meat. We get the term "a cold shoulder" from that practice. I suppose if that didn't work, they'd burn the house down rather than plainly tell someone to get out.

Chapter 9

A Time to Get, and A Time to Lose

In late November, Dad rolled the wagon into the shed, scotched the wheels, and wired the shaves to log barn rafters. This signaled the time when horse and mules got a short season of rest. In spring, summer, and harvest time our mule, Kate, worked every day in the fields except Sunday. After harvest, she rested in the pasture until it was time to get winter firewood.

A Time for Every Purpose

The time came when Dad took the crosscut saw down from the barn rafters to sharpen its mighty teeth with special files. My oldest brother, Edward, shouldered the sharp saw, and he and Mama took off for the woods. Dad gathered the leather harness from the gear room and then went to fetch Kate. Walking into the pasture, Dad caught her by the halter and then led her to the barn. He checked her teeth, feet, and ears, assuring himself that she was in good health.

Slowly he worked a sugarcoated metal bit into her reluctant mouth. Usually the mule backed away and flinched.

"WHOA KATE!" echoed about the home place.

Next, he slid a worn bridle over her ears, and then buckled it into place under her neck. He tied the bridle reins to a post while he strapped a U- shaped, padded collar in place around her neck. Next, he swung the harness onto her back, then straightened and buckled it to the collar. Moving to the rear of the mule, he pulled her tail free from the end strap. Slowly, he loosed the trace chains from the end of the harness and hooked them to the singletree with a swivel attached to it, protecting the mule in case the log rolled. He swapped the cotton plow lines on the harness for twenty-two-foot long leather check lines that would not snag on roots and rocks as she pulled heavy logs. Wrapping the check lines around his callused hands, he gently flicked Kate's side with the lines, saying, "Git up!"

The two of them headed into the woods to the site where Mama and Edward had timber on the ground ready for the mule to pull to the wood yard.

Crosscut Saw and Edward

Edward now recalls, "First, I'd chop a wedge out in the base of the tree, then sink the blade as deep as I could in the cut. The handle would point the direction the tree would fall.

"You couldn't pull a crosscut saw with Dad because he would ride the handles. That meant extra work on the other end of the saw. Mama and I had the rhythm figured out. We could cut faster than a chain saw today. Usually we felled five or six trees, then cut them into eight-foot logs. It's hard work. I've blooded my knees a many of a time pulling a crosscut saw all day long.

"We didn't trim any limbs off, so there was no brush to fool with. Dad backed the mule up to a log, hitched her up, and dropped the check lines. Kate went by herself to the wood yard where brother Ellis waited to unhook the mule and lead her back to the

A Time for Every Purpose

cutting site. Once all the logs were snaked out of the woods, Mama and I cut the trees into three foot sections of firewood and Ellis busted them. The brush was used for cook stove wood. If it got wet we'd stack it in the oven to dry it out so breakfast would cook faster."

When the chore of "snakin out firewood" ended, Dad walked the sweaty mule back to the barn and put her in a stall away from cold winds. We all knew a good work mule like Kate was vital to our survival.

A time to get and a time to lose is like everything else. It's a cycle that runs on faith.

Tom & Ada Kelly Farm
"For I saw that there is nothing better than that a man rejoices in his work, for that is his heritage." —Ecclesiastes 3:22

My Appalachian people are from a hardworking stock of Scots Irish who lived in harmony with the gifts of nature. Our heritage was woven from respect for the fact that these mountains had the power to give or take life and that if you lived in balance with these hills, their bounty always proved to be plentiful. Mountain folks were provided for and had all we needed to live on from using the skills passed down from generation to generation.

Our Appalachian parent culture was without possessions, but far richer than my generation will ever know. The once touchable solace is largely replaced by a fast-paced world.

No longer do we need to tote spring water into the house or make lye soap. Kerosene lamps gather dust on antique shelves as a reminder of dim flickers of the past. Old horse collars surround decorative mirrors and remnants of moonshine stills became yard ornaments. Industry replaced the family farms and did away with bartering. Professional transplants brought better health care, replacing home remedies. Old ways of life have vanished from the people who outgrew them. There is little need for self-sufficiency and community dependence, and that is the chief reason we don't know our neighbors anymore. Our present culture has lost its uniqueness that separated itself from others.

New generations require comfortable homes with thermostats on the wall, entertainment centers, restaurants, clothing stores, shopping centers, and golf courses. Cell phones, iPods, and computers are the world's great distractions. Our grandchildren will never plow with a mule or pull fodder in the fields, but they are wise in other ways that I know little about.

A Time for Every Purpose

Susie Tanner Swanson is a native of Murphy, North Carolina. Life as she and I once knew it is a fading patch on a quilt stitched with golden threads. Susie drew ink from her mountain heart to write of an age gone by in her book, *Echoes of Time:*

"There's nothing ever worth losing,
everything has its own place
Having served its purpose well,
with pride, dignity and grace
Time can't destroy the beauty for
as long as memory lives
Years can't erase the pleasure
to a grateful heart it gives
I'll leave it all behind me,
old, yet fresh as the dawn
Cheerful and warm for many a soul,
long after I'm gone"

Susie said, "The once tall mountains, tall enough to reach the sky have now turned into clearing landscapes with unfamiliar pathways. I still hear those old familiar echoes and my heart leads me back to that simple time. I write them down for the future generations to see what I've seen and go where I've gone, if only in their hearts and minds. Our heritage lives on in the hearts who lived and loved it."

Can you think of a better reason for Susie to write her book?

Here in the Georgia Mountains, the Foxfire program took shape and became a joint effort between young students and community elders to preserve our history, heritage, and culture for future generations. No one knew at the time that Foxfire's glow and value would spread around the world.

Volumes of stories magically became a series of twelve Foxfire Books. Today, there are more than nine million Foxfire books in print. Eventually, royalties from the Foxfire books and magazines grew and enough money was saved to purchase land in Mountain City that was rougher than a corncob.

Several original buildings were bought and reconstructed by the hands of high school students on the side of that mountain. It became The Foxfire Museum & Heritage Center that stands memorial to Appalachia's lost culture that pioneered America's first frontier. Foxfire is the centerpiece of what so many of us still hold dear. It provides a rare glimpse into a way of life that is long gone.

Meanwhile, Appalachia remains "hidden America." I am grateful and treasure the footprints of my ancestors and time spent in our simple life.

Chapter 10

A Time to Keep, and A Time to Cast Away

Recently I visited the stompin' ground of my friend and publisher, Amy Ammons Garza in the Tuckasegee community in Jackson County, North Carolina. She has deep roots in Appalachia and works hard to keep our heritage alive.

I wanted to visit some of the places Amy wrote about in her books, so I took off to a land of great solace. The deeper I walked into the woods, the quieter it got. Along the way tender green leaves pierced through dead leaves as the song of spring sweetened greening forests with thousands of wildflowers that nodded a welcome along the path.

Sitting on a rock in the bottom of a deep valley laced with pure nature, the only sound I heard was the friendly voice of a peaceful stream and occasionally the beating of pheasant wings.

My thoughts turned to Amy's folks who pioneered Jackson County. Storytelling is just one of her many talents. This one came to life as I was sitting near the very places it all happened. It's a keeper.

"Uncle Bryson told about the night Sterlen took him coon huntin' on Wolf Mountain, over past the chinquapin grove, up close to that great drop off cliff of Horseshoe Rock. . . when a storm blew up.

Bryson: "The moon was a shining a little bit when we left. It was no time until them coon hounds of Sterlen's was a' singing. Them huntin' dogs of Sterlen's weren't much good, not like my ole Blue Tick, Babe. Babe would've waited fore she'd hollowed her lungs out. I remarked on that to Sterlen. He weren't paying me no mind. I had done swapped huntin' tales with Sterlen and all them Owens boys back there at the cabin. Well they had tole me to put up or shut up. Heck, I was just a humoring Sterlen anyway. They weren't no good coons on Wolf Mountain. I knowed that.

"Well, weren't long 'til we crossed over Dogwood Hollow Springs, trottin', slow like. The dogs were still a tryin' to tree that coon or whatever it was. We'd brung a lantern with us. I had it gripped in the crook of my arm. I had both hands on the gun a toting it in front of me. All's to once, them coon dogs took off on a different tune. It shore was purdy. I started to thank maybe Sterlen's dogs wasn't all that bad after all.

"That's when the storm hit. There we was, coming up on the crest of Horseshoe and the moon done quit shining. It was just like somebody went sishhhhh and blew the moon out and tossed a dipper of water in our faces. Sterlen, he keeps a traveling but he calls out to me through the trail of thunder. 'Bryson, all that coon's a'doing is aggravating them dogs. I best take a shortcut.' He warn't to a mind for an answer.

"He dropped off down in the trees and was soon lost to me and I just kept following the sound of them dogs, straight up toward Horseshoe Rock. I was of the opinion that Sterlen done had left me on my own. Then it got darker, 'cepting for them flashes of lightnin' that looked for the world like the blinking of an old hoot owl's eyes.

"It wasn't raining too hard, just enough to get some slick on the dead leaves in the trail and a shine on them that kept slappin' on my face. By the sounds up ahead I could tell the dogs was a' baring down on that treed coon. All to onced them coon dogs hushed. There weren't no sound at all. I stopped to git my b'arings. I listened fer the dogs and fer Sterlen.

"Shore 'nough I heard Sterlen hollering somewhere up ahead. I started to move but I heard something high in them old pine limbs above me- a little bit of scratching – maybe claws on wood. I take my time and look up, right into two big staring eyes! I swallered hard and throwed out my gun there. . . steady. . .steady. . .and then I hauled off and shot that bugger's eyes out. He dropped down over to the side of the trail.

"Sterlen lets out a holler. I hollered back. Then I made my blunder, for I stepped out to lower my lantern to see what I done kilt, and my foot hit a slick spot. Boys, I moved on, and I mean moved on! My feet went out from under me and I sit down hard on the slickest rock I'd seen since Grandma dumped dirty dishwater out the winder on Daddy's bald head. I flew down that mountain! I thought for the world I'd done fell off the cleft of Horseshoe Rock! My britches got real hot, real quick. They shore 'nough had to be on fire. I just knowed my tailbone was a leaving a trail of smoke, but the Lord was a watching out for me . This rock all of a sudden throwed me out onto a branch of some sort. Stuck me like a walking stick, face first in the mud. And that gun of mine must a' been following me down that rock cause that stock of it hits me in the tail and wouldn't you know it, goes off – BOOM! Scared me out of ten years growth.

"Lord, I'd be here all night telling all the trouble I got into when I clumb outa that mud and outa that hole I done fell into. Sterlen like to have never found me. We was hoarse as bullfrogs 'fore it was all over.

"But when I finally pulled my aching bones up over that bank, there was Sterlen a' holding a ring tailed coon in my face. 'Well,' he crocked out, laughing and corhorting around. 'Whilst you were a playing on that sliding board, I been a coon huntin!'

"Boys, I could've socked him one. I wasn't feeling none too good, specially in the back side. And he was a flinging coon blood in my face! I throwed up my fist, squared off and told him to put 'em up.

"Now you know what that Sterlen done? He stopped and sobers up, a looking at me kinda quare like. Then he laughs and tells me that he ain't never believed all my bragging about what a good shot I was, but now he done changed his mind. 'You gotta be the best shot in all of Wolf Mountain,' he said. 'This coon is yorn. You got that coon right smack 'tween the eyes on the first shot. Found him here on the ground by the lantern.'

A Time for Every Purpose

"I stared, and then I turned off to head off home a smiling. 'Sterlen,' I said over my shoulder, 'It weren't that first shot, it was that second one. I shot that bugger from the bottom of that ravine, backwards!'"

The mountains are full of magnificient tales that would be lost forever if not kept alive by folks like Amy. Amy's authenticity is very refreshing in this cluttered world filled with five-dollar words and much confusion.

Bryson Ammons

Mama hated clutter. Two or three times a year she had big casting away events that she called burning spells. Items in our home could almost be found with your eyes closed. She had a few what-nots and doodads, but mostly she regarded them as dust catchers. Old clothes and shoes along with everything else not put in its place or nailed down was collected and thrown into a roaring fire in the pasture. A thick heavy smoke arose and circled the sky.

Granny Lou looked out her tiny window and said, "Lord, have mercy, Cleo is breakin' up housekeeping again. Goodness, it looks like she's going off on another train!"

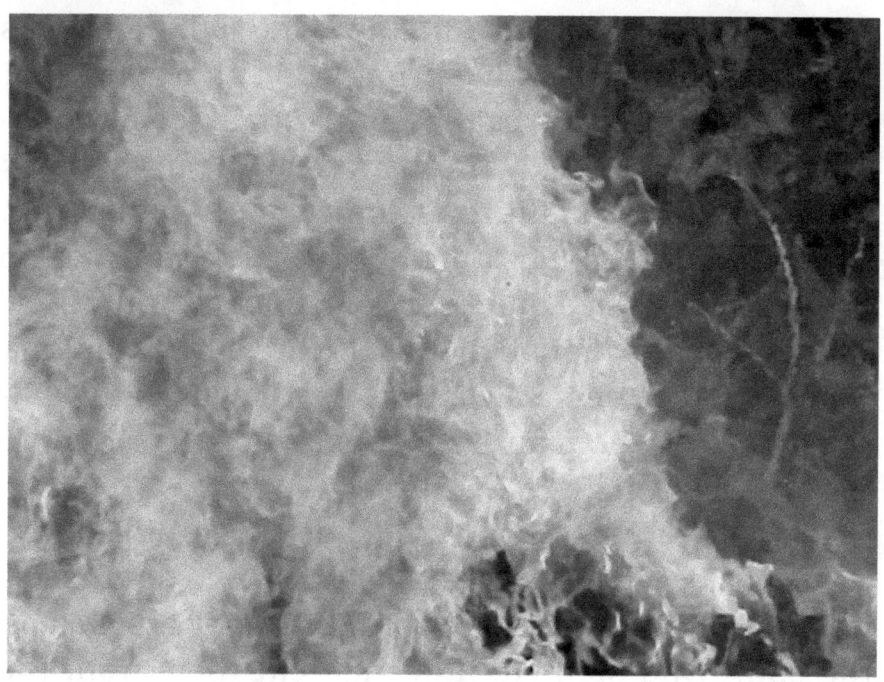

After Mama rid the home place of clutter and junk, she usually caught The Tallulah Falls Railroad to Franklin, NC, to visit folks. The twenty mile round trip ticket cost ten cents. She was born and reared in

A Time for Every Purpose

the Skeenah community. "Skeenah" is a Cherokee word. According to several sources, it means "ghost" or "the abode of Satan." I wonder if she knew the meaning because often she jested, "The farther you went up Skeenah th' meaner they got. We lived at th' end of the road."

As the train crawled north from the station in Dillard, we watched as the little red caboose slowly faded out of sight, You could walk and keep up with it. Mama jested it was so slow that one fellow gave up waiting on the train and decided to commit suicide by laying down on the track. He starved to death before the train arrived.

About the only casting away done by Dad was barn manure onto early spring fields as fertilizer for spring planting. I never thought I'd ever see cow manure sold in stores. My brothers cleaned out livestock stalls, piling the manure at the edge of the pasture. Here, it went through "a heat" process, and it had to be turned often. Chemical reactions could cause spontaneous combustion that Kelly's Creek couldn't water out. The heat killed some weed seeds in the manure. Drying the manure made it easier to cast onto the waiting fields.

Mule-drawn sleds were loaded then pulled into the fields, because a wagon might tip over. Its runners were made from sourwood poles that grew crooked on the end. Dad spotted, and then cut them from the woods. He measured and sawed two poles into six-foot lengths for the runners, and then he shaped both poles with a chopping ax and a draw knife. Next, he bored three holes in the top of each runner with his brace-n-bit. He cut six standards about two feet long to fit the holes. Oak boards rested against the standards to hold cargo on the sled. The floor was crude oak boards. He continued boring holes between the crooked runners to attach chains and a singletree that was hooked to the mule.

Granny Lou called horse and mule manure "hoss biscuits." She kept a manure apron hanging on a nail in the barn. In the spring, she filled one pocket with "hoss biscuits" and the other with seed corn.
As she dug holes to plant, she dropped one "hoss biscuit" and one grain of corn. Each seed was vital. She knew it took eleven acres of corn to feed one cow year round.

My brothers, Edward and Ellis, worked many days broadcasting the fields. Ellis said, "One day Edward worked fast t' get through before 5:00 in hopes of going a few miles t' Dillard for moon pies and soda dopes. We jumped on the mule and turned in at Greenwood Lane, where a rattling bridge crossed the Little Tennessee River. The bridge looked like a stock gate, so when the mule saw the water it balked. Finally, I pulled off my shirt and tied it over the mule's eyes then led her across. On we went towards Dillard, dreaming of moon pies. I got to thinking, what if the Tallulah Falls Train comes in and scares the mule? A skeered mule might cover the town broadcasting its own hot manure! So, I hid th' mule behind Ferman Vinson's store."

Chapter 11

A Time to Rend, and a Time to Sew

The saints of old tore their garments as an outward sign of the condition of their hearts during times of sorrow. The great book of Joel states to rend our hearts and not our garments. Rending the heart is a painful thing, especially one steeped in traditions. I once believed repentance meant laying hold of car bumpers on bended knee engulfed with guilt and shame for things like smoking, staying out all night, not going to church or painted fingernails. Until the appointed time to rend my heart of pre-conceived religious beliefs, I was stuck in the bondage of programed religion. The process of changing my mind tore me to pieces. It took a lot of divine sewing to mend my prior thinking and beliefs.

Coming out of religious bondage made me want to help others bound by chains that bind and choke true Christianity.

During a rainy Wednesday night meeting of the faithful in a nearby church, the subject of discussion were rules that govern church leaders, deacons, counsel men, and teachers. The pastor read from 1 Timothy Chapter 3: *"A bishop then must be blameless, the husband of one wife, vigilant, sober, of good behavior, given to hospitality, apt to teach;"*

He stated in order to hold an office in their church all the above must be enforced. A discussion followed about divorce. A young man in his mid-30s sat with his family near a window pounded by hard rain. He stood up, cleared his throat, and asked to speak. I sensed nervous tension in his voice as he said, "My heart's desire is to hold the office of teacher here. I was legally divorced and re-married two years ago. I feel that I qualify because I am the husband of one wife."

I sensed his longing to be of service. Someone on the back pew replied that according to the Bible, the young man was living in adultery since his first wife was living. My heart sank like an anchor in troubled waters. Raising my hand, I asked if divorce was the unpardonable sin?

The young man sat back down.

The pastor said, "No, but there are consequences, like being forbidden to hold offices in church. I'm the authority here and it is my personal conviction and the rules of this denomination that divorcees cannot hold offices"

That really bothered me. It's a sorry dog that won't bark. I felt the judgment cup being poured out on divorcees in the congregation. Practicing legalism puts strings on the Cross and creates second-class Christians. The snake of legalism slithers in many mainstream church doors to use the letter of the written Word that kills as opposed to the Spirit of the

Word that gives freedom and life. Legalism is bad company; it is hard to get rid of. It is my conviction the ground is level at the Cross.

Now that I had stirred up a hornet nest, I felt compelled to finish my thoughts. I asked if they were aware that we served a divorced Father?

Tension grew tigher than a banjo string.

Next, I read a marked verse in my Bible from Jeremiah Chapter 3 verse 8: *"And I saw, when for all the causes whereby backsliding Israel committed adultery I had put her away, and gave her a bill of divorce; yet her treacherous sister Judah feared not, but went and played the harlot also."*

In short, idol worship caused God to divorce two spiritual wives. I concluded with, "According to your doctrine, Christ will return someday to marry again at the marriage supper of the Lamb. Does that mean He cannot hold an office here?"

No one answered. A deep silence fell over the people, and then someone changed the subject.

I was reminded of a story a friend told me that was meant to be funny: "An old timer was standing on the street corner with his hands resting inside the bib of his blue overalls. A newcomer approached the old timer asking, "Where is the church of God around here?" The old-timer thought a moment then said, 'Well, Jack Rigors has got one over yonder past th' lake, and Andrew Hardy has one north of here, now let me think... There are several going west, but, naw, I don't think God has one around here."

Divorce and other rends in our earthly journey happen. In my day, divorce rarely occurred but when it did, folks referred to separated couples as having "split' th' blanket."

Brother Ellis said, "You never heard of such until the shirt factory come here giving women jobs outside the home. I guess jobs gave them more independence. With th' mixin' of people, there usually comes some trouble. Course th' first divorce I heard about was in 1949. A feller returned from the war and learned his wife had been unfaithful so they 'split th' blanket."

~ ~ ~

Mountaineers made their own blankets and cloth on the farm. Some owned a few sheep that produced enough wool to supply needs. Sheep were often free-ranged. The owners marked them with a notch in each animal's ear to identify ownership, and then registered that mark at the courthouse. A healthy sheep grew two teeth a year. One with eight teeth was four years old. When they lost their teeth, they quit producing wool.

A Time for Every Purpose

At an appointed time, the sheep were sheared. The wool was gathered, washed, and then combed with cards into soft bats for spinning. The spun threads was used for knitting, sewing, and weaving. Granny Lou's spinning wheel buzzed like bees building a nest as she turned the giant wheel with her right hand while holding pieces of fiber in her left hand. Carefully she guided the fibers around a revolving spindle that stored the yarn attached to the spinning wheel. Thousands of yarn threads were laced into looms for weaving cloth. Walnut hulls, onions, roots, and berries were chopped, boiled in water, and used for dye. The whole process was time consuming but rewarding in warm clothing.

The looms of life never stop creating patterns that mark our journey. Sometimes we encounter and work through knots and broken strands in the process, but the finished work of God's tapestry is perfect. It was a miraculous process from blades of tender grass growing in peaceful pastures, to the humble sheep producing wool, to the hands that made blankets and clothing.

Everything that sustains our bodies can be traced back to mother earth.

I have never sewed too much and am probably the only woman fired from the shirt factory labeled unable to sew. One of the few times I paid attention in home economics class, I learned the basics.

Jean Nelson is an avid seamstress. She said, "I remember sitting down to the sewing machine with sweaty palms. It was like I had been reborn. My first project was a little doggie face pillow. Back then, a pattern was $.25, and the fabric was $.25. I was in heaven at the cotton shop.

"I had a no nonsense teacher in home economics class. She made me remove my collar from my shirt-dress seven times. I was fearful the dress would be worn out before it was finished. I had offended her by sharing how to put a zipper in much easier than what she taught.

"Towards the end of school, I cleaned out my locker and took my supplies home. The day of our final exam, I did not have a needle for hand sewing to complete the exam. I went to her and asked if I could borrow a needle and I guess she chose to teach me a lesson and would not let me take my exam. I checked the list she made for needed supplies for the test, but a needle was not on it. That was the only time Mom went to school on my behalf, but I got to take the exam that afternoon. I was never interested in home economics class after that.

"I had a taste for fashion that couldn't be satisfied in a clothing store. I loved bold and bright colors. Sewing allowed me to be me. It was a very big part of my life and afforded a great sense of accomplishment. I made the children's' clothes and sold fabric crafts for about twenty-five years through consignment shops and craft fairs."

Granny Lou took many stitches in her lifetime, quietly working with her hands. She said sewing is good nerve medicine. When life threw handfuls of uneven scraps, she made warm quilts to cover her hard-

A Time for Every Purpose

ships. She forbid sewing on Sunday saying, "Every stitch you take on Sunday, you will remove with your nose someday." Well-placed stitches in life afford rest from labors. Hems with love never ravel.

When our clothing needed to be patched or mended, a time to sew was in order at our house. A much-used red metal fruitcake box with a Christmas scene lid sat tightly closed above Mama's bed on a shelf that was out of our reach. Her treasure box contained needles, threads, and colored buttons of all sizes, scissors, thimbles, and a pincushion that looked like a small tomato.

After she sorted shirts and britches for mending, she carefully lifted the red box from a splintered shelf and carried it to the light of a window for better sight. She selected a spool of sewing thread, then pulled a strand about two feet long before breaking it off at the spool. Next she chose a shiny needle that she held in her left hand.

Touching her pointer finger to her tongue, she wet the end of the thread by twirling it between her thumb and finger to smooth the frayed ends. Holding the needle at eye-level, she then began to push the thread through the eye of the needle. After she pulled the thread through the needle, she again wet her finger, before tying a knot in the end of the thread to make it hold the mend tightly in place.

She cut and placed matching patches as best she could on torn garments. Then she baste stitched the patch in place. Much later in life I thought about the lessons of fixing rends.

If only we would reach into the treasure box of our heart, move into the Light with silver needles of forgiveness and golden threads of love, our differences would be mended.

Lastly, if we tied a knot in our efforts the mend would not ravel.

Mrs. Edith Darnell, beloved Foxfire contact
The Foxfire Museum and Heritage Center. www.foxfire.org

Chapter 12

A Time to Keep Silent, and A Time to Speak

They say silence is golden, but it also comes in many colors in the Georgia mountains. I covet silence among maiden ferns and wild flowers wet with morning dew. I watch silent movements of dormant creatures finding their way through a jungle of plants that covers the forest floor and teachs me how to navigate around, over or underneath hard obstacles along life's paths.

Laurel thickets with white round blooms against green leaves remind me of Christmas in July.

In autumn, a deep stillness settles on fenceless trails only broken by falling acorns and hickory nuts that strip leaves on changing trees. Nature's clock ticks as the sun's thermostat is turned down. Sometime in early December, fresh snow begins to pepper from the heavens, like a mighty righteous army covering the ground in a white pristine gown. It cloaks rocks, logs, and slopes in graceful mounds. As the snow falls in countless flakes, the air is cleansed and the stains on earth's surfaces are covered. All the forest becomes still again as a strange silence fills the air that causes one to walk softly through crystal halls. The withered flowers of summer seem to return as white jewels. The mountains write their own poetry.

Silence is the forbearance of speech. It is a time to be still and embrace times of peace. Inward stillness affords the soul a time of rest from confusion and demands of fleshly needs. Silence is the absence of tribulations.

We have the silence of the night, yet the wind

prowls through the treetops, rustling leaves and branches where owls hoot from far away. Gentle trickles of a mountain spring run through moss-covered rocks with a still voice of their own.

Stillness without distractions allows me to hear God. He speaks in many ways; in fact, He is always speaking. If I am not plugged in to spiritual frequency I cannot hear His Voice. Our heart is an earthly receiver. A mistuned radio gives only static. What good is a television satellite attached to the house without a receiver inside?

Often I am caught up in voicing my own concerns too much. Once I prayed fervently for a dear friend. Repeatedly, I pleaded with God to heal the afflictions that kept her bound. As I sat by the creek waters, my focus turned to a single leaf trapped in the current among rocks. As it spun around and around I knew it was a picture of my prayers. I learned that I must let go.

Later my friend said, "If God never does another thing for me, He has done enough."

Many lessons abound. Young Christopher gets scrapes and scuffs playing outside. Immediately he cries for my attention to fix them. His distress delays close inspection and healing. Therefore, it is sometimes like that with God and me.

There is also a deafening negative silence that not only stops ears but also lives when we sometimes choose silence over speaking out.

~ ~ ~

The mountains are not immune to domestic abuse. A time to speak increased when people acquired enough courage to report abuse. Still, many others among us suffer in silence with no voice, like caged, crippled birds in a home prison: Steel doors seem locked; the abused have no wings, and they have no song.

I had no idea how widespread domestic abuse was in my county before volunteering at a local abuse shelter. My heart sank for victims caught in the endless cycle with no strength to break out. Icy walls seem too thick to chisel through.

I was on call the afternoon of July 4 when I was alerted of a crisis needing my attention. At the county jail sat a young woman slumped over in pain. Her thin blonde hair was stained with blood, her voice broken and her body shaking uncontrollably. After an embrace, I noticed burns around her mouth. She told me the fight with her boyfriend started in the yard and continued to the woodshed where he pinned her down, then fed her live cigarette burning butts. I was horrified. Those who work with the abused are always horrified; that is why they fervently work to change situations and ease pain. Both activists, social workers and victims take deep breaths, close their eyes, and pray for a better tomorrow that usually never comes until action is taken to end the cycle of abuse.

A voice is a very powerful vehicle of freedom whether in the moment of necessity or as a means of helping those trapped in the vortex of abuse. A time to speak can be the answer to someone's prayer. We can make a difference in a few lives. Volunteer, donate, or extend an olive branch of support. At least offer a warm embrace, but please do not be silent. If ever there is an appointed time to speak, this is one of them. Speaking out takes courage and is a chief form of love.

Abuse comes in many forms. The most recent environmental issue is exploration for natural gas using hydraulic fracking to extract fossil fuels. Those who love Appalachia have a long history of speaking out on environmental issues.

The greatest concern with fracking is contamination of ground water with unknown blends of toxic chemicals used in the process. Pipeline explosions, wastewater disposal, and an increase in earthquakes are also concerns raised in voices of opposition. But like the coal mining companies that raped central Appalachia for generations and destroyed the landscapes with mountain top removal, the fracking industry takes no heed to the outcries of the activists. It is a matter of dollars, and many regard fracking as a way to produce more oil and reduce fuel costs in the end. Fracking is also thought to be a great source of jobs for Appalachia. People do not want to toy with livelihoods.

Beware of those who praise Appalachia's natural goldmines for gain. Beware of those who promise environmental safety and jobs. Such is of no value to dead people. When clean air, fresh water, and healthy soil are gone, so are we. It is up to good stewards of

the earth to care for natural gifts. Environmental awareness is necessary for life itself.

I fear history books will record that a few voiced complaints, a few wrote letters and a few stood in protest lines. Perhaps it will read that little was done to stop fracking as wild animals died and streams be-

A Time for Every Purpose

came contaminated and the blessed earth soaked up the poisons. The new generations glow in the dark from drinking water laced with chemicals, but their utility bills are lower. Droves of folks looked for a safe place to live and found none. Mostly done in the name of jobs. What th' FRACK have we done!

Chapter 13

A Time to Love, and A Time to Hate

The simplest and most profound statement of the ages is "God is love." A simple snowglobe is a picture of God's sealing and protection of His children in the round world. We are like the swirling snowflakes often caught in life's storms that occur within His perfect circle. Sometimes we swirl around with no direction. Sometimes we stick to the side of the globe before settling to the bottom, bonding with countless other flakes. Nothing we might do can ever separate us from His perfect circle of love. People have failed to completely define love because no one can completely define God. Once embraced, it is the only power that changes lives. We are governed by either law or love. If law could change hearts, prisons would be empty.

I suppose the chief season for expressing love is during Christmas. Our hearts wrap memories like neat packages that are opened over and over for a lifetime.

The first sign of Christmas a'comin' in our mountain home was Mama opening a big can of

A Time for Every Purpose

Johnson's paste wax to smear all over the plank floors, then waiting for my brother and me to get home from school. The smell of wax ensured the house would turn into a fun skating rink. Our skates were thick wool socks knitted by Granny Lou. We slipped, slid, giggled, and wiggled for hours, polishing the floors. That was the first shine of the season.

About a week before Christmas Eve, my brother and I gathered up brown tow sacks and a double bitted ax and began a journey by foot three miles away to Littleton Cove where a grove of cedar trees grew. We wrapped up in scarves and coats and pulled tattered toboggans over our ears to cross fields and dales cold and white. Heavy frost looked like a young snow and sparkled like diamonds in the golden sunlight. The frozen forest bed crunched like walking on dry corn shucks. When we stopped to rest, the only sound was our deep breaths mixed with cold air and formed steam. All nature seemed to stand still in a holy hush that could not be described with words, only felt deep within.

Straddling an old fence, we journeyed onward with the hope of finding red and green Christmas treasures to fill our sacks. In the distance, faint glimpses of red holly berries and green branches encouraged us in our quest. Soon our sacks began to bulge as we stuffed nature's treasures inside. We paused a moment, playing with holly leaves that were easily turned into toys when held between the thumb and forefinger. We blew hard breaths on them, creating entertaining flutter mills.

Once a tree was located, Ernest made me bend the tree over while he swung the ax. He knew the jarring of the cedar tree would cause its limbs to scratch me like cat claws, so he chopped a while and laughed a while as an eternity seemed to pass before it finally fell to the ground. Our sacks loaded with burrs, berries and boughs, and the tree in tow, we started home.

Mama tied two colored ropes across the porch to display our collections of decorations. Inside she twisted green pine branches with colorful Galax leaves into pretty wreaths to scent the house. As she worked, she sang Christmas songs. One was about a Star of hope and rest that guided the wise men on their way to find Jesus. She said, "The Bible says when they entered into the house they saw the young child first, and all the rest second. I wished I had seen Him first instead of a bunch of religion." She told of precious gifts of gold, frankincense, and myrrh that lay before Him.

At night, we busied ourselves talking about Christmas and making colorful chains from strips cut out of the Sears and Roebuck catalogue. The links were held together with glue made from flour and water. Collected chestnut burrs and pinecones were rolled in the remaining mixture to turn them into white balls for the tree.

Ernest cracked black walnuts with a hammer, and then picked out the meat by the light of the fireplace for Christmas goodies while I cut paper snowflakes to hang on the windowpanes. Moonbeams shown through the paper holes, creating golden patterns on the walls adding to Christmas magic. Prince Albert tobacco cans were cut in strips and used for icicles, and silver stars were shaped out of foil from old cigarette pack linings. Stars reminded me of the one seen by the wise men.

Dad said, "You have to be wise to know where to look in the heavens."

After the tree was tied to a corner wall, it was ready for us to begin hanging the decorations. Meanwhile, sweet smells filtered from the kitchen to make us more anxious for Christmas to come.

On Christmas Eve, Dad took the Bible off the mantel after supper and read the old story about baby Jesus lying in a manger. He said the bread of life was put in a feeding trough to feed the world, and especially on Christmas Eve when the cattle in the barn got down on their knees in remembrance. Our eyes widened with amazement, and Ernest said, "Let's go see!" He lit the lantern and we took off towards the barn in the cold night to peek through wide cracks. Sure enough, the cows were lying down in the soft hay.

When we returned to the crackling warm fire inside the house, sister Bea, a first grader, was hanging three wool socks above the fireplace and singing a song she learned in class: *"What can I give Him, poor as I am? If I were a shepherd, I'd give Him a lamb. If I were a wise man, I'd do my part; yet what can I give Him, I'll give Him my heart."*

Dad said, "Let's act like the cattle and kneel down; let's offer our hearts too." Simple prayers mixed with the sweet smells from the kitchen ascended upward. Christmas Eve in the calm, silent mountains ended.

The next day, three excited young'uns jumped up early to see what Santa Claus brought. Our socks were filled with stick candy, rag dolls, slingshots, crow calls, whistles, apples, oranges, and a few funny looking nuts. Finally, Mama said, "Run to the woodshed! I heard a rustle out there and th' dog raised cain all night. Santa Claus might have stopped there."

Sure enough, he did, and he left a red wagon with sideboards and two store bought dolls. Christmas dawn was just breaking over the blue-hazed mountains. Ernest pulled his wagon inside near the fire. He put his pillow in the wagon, climbed in and fell asleep. This is one memory I will continue to unwrap year after year in my heart.

Children can give unconditional love before they are taught to hate. In late October, 1980, I was raking colorful leaves in the yard into piles as our two-year old daughter giggled and jumped into the soft mounds. Her golden hair was laced with twigs and crushed leaves. I became distracted by the chore and did not notice she had disappeared from sight. I began calling her name and frantically searching high and low. She did not answer and fear paralyzed my mind. Minutes seemed to turn into hours as my heartbeat-measured time.

I soon discovered she was quietly playing on the sandy bank behind the house totally absorbed in her young imagination. Instead of being overjoyed to find my lost lamb, anger arose inside me and burned like a fire. Anger is a form of insanity. I grabbed her by the arms yelling, "Why didn't you answer me!" Then, I opened the back door and roughly pushed her down the hallway towards her room. Her happy eyes turned into deep pools of sadness as she experienced fear. She crawled onto her bed crying, not having a clue what she had done wrong. Each time I passed by her room she reached for me in a loving manner. Her error was innocent, like many of mine. That was the first time I experienced unconditional love as a parent.

Finally, we embraced in hugs that formed circles of love. It was a powerful lesson. There is always a time to love. The opposite of love is hate and there is an appointed time for this.

~ ~ ~

God hates evil doing and the twisted darkness that is the source of it. We are told in the Bible to hate evil acts, not the person. One example of evil acts is addictions that begin as a little choice but progress into a big deadly habit. Millions of families are affected by substance abuse. Mine is not exempt. The national cost of substance abuse cannot compare to the cost of family breakdowns. We have felt the sting of addicts feeding their weakness by lying, cheating, conning, and stealing. Mind altering substances separate victims from reality as drugs and alcohol become gods.

There is a unique word in the Bible that pertains to illegal drug use. Revelation 21:8: *"But the fearful, and unbelieving, and the abominable, and murderers, and whoremongers, and sorcerers, and idolaters, and all liers, shall have their part in the lake which burneth with fire...."*

The word "sorcerers" is "pharmakeus" in Greek. It is where we get our word, pharmacy. It is talking about drug dealers, not the medical profession.

I believe the lake of fire is God Himself *"Our God is a consuming fire."* —Hebrews 12:29.

At an appointed time, He melts away our imperfections and hate shall vanish. A good example of change is a tree. By a sharpened ax, it becomes a log. The log is placed on a fire where it changes to ashes. Ashes are wood that has changed form. Likewise, we are changed into new creatures.

Chapter 14

A Time of War, and A Time of Peace

War machines come in the form of hunting dogs in the mountains. Dogs were vital additions to our family, not only to find meat but also to defend the homeland and keep the peace. Ol' Nell, our black and tan coon dog, spent most of her days in a box of hay under the porch, curled up tighter than a girdle on a preacher's wife. She appeared to be very slow and lazy until her big floppy ears and wet nose detected possums in the corncrib or foxes sneaking around the hen house. First a thump came from under the porch as she banged her head on a post hurrying to the task, and then a looong, loud alarm like a trumpet pierced the air, sending us rushing out to investigate. A war was on.

Ol' Nell was never aggressive toward people, except the time the undertaker (whose hearse doubled as the county's ambulance) came to pick up Aunt Ruth during one of her occasional fainting spells. It had snowed the night before, and the ground and our front steps were covered with ice. He backed the hearse as close as he could to the house, opened the rear door, then slipped and slid through the yard. Ol' Nell banged her head on a post, then sounded the alarm. Mama was first responder with the broom in her hand, but not quick enough to stop Ol' Nell. The dog went straight for the seat of the man's britches. Mama scolded Ol' Nell and kept her at bay until he was inside the house.

The undertaker/ambulance driver rolled Aunt Ruth onto the lowered stretcher, strapped her in place, and began rolling her down the icy steps. Midway down, Ol' Nell made a second attack. The man abandoned the stretcher, and Aunt Ruth went bumping alone down the slick steps. At the bottom the stretcher overturned, throwing Aunt Ruth into the snow.

The sight was beyond funny. By now, Mama was between Ol' Nell and the undertaker, and Aunt Ruth was working at getting free from the stretcher straps--all the while a'cussin' Ol' Nell: "It don't cost no more to feed a sorry dog than a good one!" She was beyond disgusted and went back in the house where she poured herself some black coffee before going to bed. I don't recall that she ever had another fainting spell.

Laurie--my dear friend of forty years, intrepid editor and dog lover--loves to share her experience with hunting dogs.

"The first of February, 2011, I moved into a small cabin where I would spend the following spring and summer, high on a ridge in the beautiful mountains of northeast Georgia. The side of the mountain ridge that held the cabin paralleled another heavily wooded mountain ridge, and the two mountains formed a cove. Barbara, her husband Larry, and their fine Redtick hound Charlie lived just below me. Barbara's brother, his wife, and their hunting beagles Joe and Jack lived farther down, near the entrance to the cove. When I was on my porch early one morning shortly after moving in, I noticed Charlie quietly watching me from a distance. I called to him, and he came closer. I called him again, and he slowly stepped up onto the porch. When I put my hand on his head and told him how glad, I was to see him, gallant Charlie became my loyal friend.

"I enjoyed my canine neighbors. Charlie visited early every morning and often in the evening before the sun went down. The two beagles ran past my cabin just after dawn each morning, noses to the ground, on a mission to seek out and track whatever wildlife signs they could find up and over the ridge. I kept a stainless steel pot of fresh water on my porch, and they generally meandered back down around noontime and stopped in for a drink and a brief greeting before heading home.

"One night in early March, I awoke to the distant sound of dogs warring against something near the top of the mountain ridge. The word 'war' means a state of armed conflict, and unexpected mountain soldiers in the form of four-legged infantry fought this one. As I focused on the racket, I identified Charlie's sustained baritone and the beagles' high-pitched yelps. Briefly wondering why they were so excited, I turned over and went back to sleep. A couple of days later, I discovered what was unmistakably a bear track just a couple hundred yards up from the cabin. Hibernating bears were beginning to stir about, I reasoned.

"It was in May and June that our cove became the target of a wave of night-roaming bear activity. Every couple of nights I would wake up hearing Charlie, Joe, and Jack fiercely confronting the intruders somewhere in the distance, but one night I awoke to hear the dogs baying and snarling with unprecedented ferocity no more than twenty yards from the cabin. The sound reverberated off the sides of the mountain ridges and came through my open window in waves that seemed surreal. As I listened and prayed fervently for the dogs' protection, I realized they were using what I termed 'hound sense': instead of attacking head-on (and getting killed or maimed with one powerful swipe), they were all three jumping in at the bear(s) and quickly dancing back out in a fiercely unrelenting barrage of threatening activity and noise that kept them just out of reach of bear paws, claws and teeth. That night our canine defense team drove the intruder all the way down the ridge and out of the cove with no damage done to persons, property, or themselves.

"The next morning I saw with my own eyes the clear signs that a large bear had been around the cabin the night before. When I praised and petted Charlie, Joe, and Jack that day, they were delighted but seemed mystified by my enthusiasm. It was then that I dubbed them 'Canine Security Force-1.'

"As bears continued to enter our cove at night, Canine Security Force-1 stepped up their surveillance

A Time for Every Purpose

from dusk to dawn. I myself made it a point to be home and inside before dark each evening, but one night I missed my self-imposed curfew by a good two hours. There was no moon, and the mountainside was totally dark. I parked in the usual spot, raced the engine a bit, turned on my little LED flashlight, and launched myself out of the car and into the inky blackness, fervently praying there were no bear cubs playing around my porch and no mama bears at hand ready and waiting to take me on.

"As I swung the flashlight back and forth before closing the car door there was a flash of red and white, and I could see Charlie's blessedly familiar form moving just beyond the light. I stood next to the car door and waited as he checked the area. When he was satisfied there was no threat, he came to my side and escorted me up the ramp onto the porch and to my front door. I gave him a quick hug and thanked him, but other than waving his tail, he did not move until I went inside and closed the door. He then vanished.

"It was around the end of the first week in July that the nights became quiet and peaceful in our cove. I gave credit where credit was due and shared the story of Canine Security Force-1 many times, never tiring of telling how one gallant Redtick hound and two courageous beagles no bigger than Jack Russell terriers defended their home place, kept the peace and turned away the bear invasion of 2011."

Blessed be the peacekeepers! At the end of any war whether it involves animals, physical combat or spiritual warfare, a time of peace follows.

Charlie—one gallant Redtick hound

There are constant wars in the earth beyond the Georgia mountains that I have absolutely no control over. What matters is controlling the wars that occur in my earth (mind) that rob me of tranquility and peace. Thoughts, ideas, and notions are like seeds germinating in a garden. Some are good seeds of beauty and some are seeds of hurtful thorns.

One thing that helps me keep peace of mind is to pay attention to negative thoughts that enter my brain. Negative thinking is a bad habit, feeding mind, body and soul with defeat. Wise Soloman said in Ecclesiastes 6:3, if man's soul is not filled with good, it is better for him to die in a miscarriage than live the life of a grump.

It helps to know where negativity comes from.

A Time for Every Purpose

Often it is my ego or an outside source tempting me to react negatively. Positive thoughts come from God's throne located within each of His children.

There is an amazing passage and a beautiful type of a processing seat in the Bible. 1 Kings Chapter 10 is for your consideration. I in no way am pushing my own beliefs.

[18] Moreover the king made a great throne of ivory, and overlaid it with the best gold [19] The throne had six steps, and the top of the throne was round behind: and there were stays on either side on the place of the seat, and two lions stood beside the stays. [20] And twelve lions stood there on the one side and on the other upon the six steps: there was not the like made in any kingdom.

A quick study of the human brain reveals the color of pale white or ivory overlaid with a reddish gold color. It is round as described above. The two lions represent the power of both positive and negative thoughts. The twelve lions that stand on the sides are types of our cranial nerves. The six steps are types of the six major parts of the brain. Certainly, our brain is a powerful computer. Nothing can compare to it. It is here we separate right from wrong, good from evil. As I believe, the earth is my brain and heaven is my heart.

Jesus said, *"I give unto thee the keys of the kingdom of heaven: and whatsoever thou shalt bind on earth shall be bound in heaven and whatsoever thou loose on earth shall be loosed in heaven."* —Matthew 16:19

If I allow negative thoughts to take root in my head, they will surely rob my peace of mind. The gospel armor spoken of by the apostle Paul in Ephesians 6 is God's provisions to keep us spiritually strong. One of the articles is shoes of peace. A soldier cannot stand with sore feet.

Conclusion

I am sure you have noticed Solomon lists twenty-eight appointed times during the cycle of life that are polar-opposites and include times of durations. Life's cycles from birth to beyond the grave are less stressful once we believe all things are controlled by God. Even when we feel like a disjointed puzzle, the pieces are pre-destined to come together in a beautiful picture.

"He hath made everything beautiful in His time: also He hath set the (eternal) world in their heart, so that no man can find out the work that God maketh from the beginning to the end." —Ecclesiastes 3:11

Note it says HIS time, not mine. The word "world" as used in the above verse means everlasting or eternal. It is written the Kingdom of God is within you. The King and His dominion cannot be seen with fleshly eyes apart from you and me. This came as an eye-opener to me one morning as I was having coffee with the Lord. We drink it black. He brings the sweetener. I started reading a passage in the book of John.

Some Greek folks outside the temple asked to see Jesus. Disciples Phillip and Andrew went to tell Him. This was His reply in part;

"Verily, verily, I say unto you, except a corn of wheat fall into the ground and die, it abideth alone: but if it die it bringeth forth much fruit." —John 12:24

I said, Lord, "That's the quarest answer I believe I've ever heard and it don't make a lick of sense to me. Perhaps I need stronger coffee."

Then my understanding was opened as I read His words again. He was the wheat that died; we are the fruit from Him. His answer means the only way the Greeks and others can see Jesus with fleshly eyes is to see Him within His children.

There are twenty-eight appointed times that are divided into fourteen lines in Ecclesiastes. I am glad man does not have the power to change any of them, for whatever man lays his hand on usually becomes a mess. Perhaps that is why man was created last on His list.

Everything is made beautiful in HIS time. Our lives were divinely chosen and pre-destined before the foundations of the world were laid. Each season brings change in a great school of learning. I have learned that prayer does not change God's mind or His plan. Prayer changes me.

He planted a good seed in every man's heart. In His appointed time, it will grow and produce good fruits. I cannot see the planned beauty deep inside an ugly seed in my hand. It is a gift to be able to look beyond germination, to beautiful flowers, and strong produce.

A Time for Every Purpose

When life hands us death, weeping, mourning, hate, and war, we have a promise of better days to come. Healing happens, laughter, dancing. peace and love returns.

Lemons of life are going to come. Some of us make lemonade and drink it ourselves. Consider making a lemonade stand to share the sweetness of our seasons with others as we wait for the reconciliation of all things.

Therefore, we see our lives come full circle. May we embrace the present time, as that is the only reality there is. It is necessary to change our minds and keep them focused on things that really matter. The longest roads in the world are yesterday and tomorrow.

Blue Valley

About the Author

Foxfire veteran and seasoned storyteller Barbara Taylor Woodall couples mountain sensibility with spiritual depth in *'A Time For Every Purpose.'* Her best-selling first book *"It's Not My Mountain Anymore"* paved the way for Woodall's Appalachian voice to reach a national audience in a segment aired on **CBS This Morning** and a worldwide audience in the BBC series **'How the Wild West Was Won with Ray Mears.'** Her deep generational roots in the north Georgia mountains are brought to light again in *"A Time For Every Purpose"* as she weaves the wit and wisdom of plain living with Biblical principles to offer simple prescriptions for life in today's world.

A Time for Every Purpose

"It's a relief to hear YOU [Barbara] talking as though you were sitting here in my living room. The end result is that one is left with the feeling that this is a person who it would be fun to know- someone who's affectionate, perceptive, loyal...and who's a great story teller. *'A Time For Every Purpose'* is a worthy addition to the little shelf that holds the Barbara Taylor Woodall materials. May it someday groan under the weight of all your insights and experiences!"

—Eliot Wigginton,
Former teacher and founder of The Foxfire Fund

For additional copies of this book, please complete on a separate sheet of paper the following details:

Name: _____

Address: _____

_____

Phone (in case of returns): _____

_____Books @ 20.00 (includes postage)

_____Total Order

Please make the check payable to Barbara Woodall.

Send check or money order to the following address:

A Time For Every Purpose
1410 Crusher Run Road
Rabun Gap, Georgia 30568

❏ I am interested in receiving more information about how to acquire Barbara Taylor Woodall as a speaker for our club or civic meeting, dinner meeting, a book signing, libraries or....

Email: shine5@windstream.net

www.ingramcontent.com/pod-product-compliance
Lightning Source LLC
Chambersburg PA
CBHW070919160426
43193CB00011B/1520